Robert Chamblet Adams

Travels in Faith

From Tradition to Reason

Robert Chamblet Adams

Travels in Faith
From Tradition to Reason

ISBN/EAN: 9783337205560

Printed in Europe, USA, Canada, Australia, Japan

Cover: Foto ©Lupo / pixelio.de

More available books at **www.hansebooks.com**

FROM

TRADITION TO REASON

BY

ROBERT C. ADAMS

"There lives more faith in honest doubt,
Believe me, than in half the creeds."
TENNYSON.

G. P. PUTNAM'S SONS
NEW YORK: 27 & 29 WEST 23D STREET
LONDON: 25 HENRIETTA ST., COVENT GARDEN
1884

CONTENTS.

		PAGE.
I.	Travels in Faith	1
II.	A Radical Avowal	71
III.	Gain or Loss?	77
IV.	Human Religion	96
V.	Is the Bible the Word of God?	105
VI.	The Bible a Human Book	115
VII.	Human Ideas of God	125
VIII.	Prayer	138
IX.	Morality	144
X.	The Future	156
XI.	The Church and its Work	168
XII.	The Decline of the Ministry	177
XIII.	The Consolations of Christianity	186
XIV.	Material Immortality	194
XV.	Liberal Convictions	197
XVI.	Reform	207
XVII.	Truth in Error	215
XVIII.	Free Thought Rhymes	236

TRAVELS IN FAITH.

I.

When Dr. Lyman Beecher was asked, "What is the best way to promote revivals?" he answered, "By telling of them." Temperance platforms, experience meetings, and the efforts of evangelists prove that the surest way to gain converts is to narrate the conversion of others. "I believed, and therefore have I spoken," has been the warrant through ages for the utterance of sincere conviction. Truth is free to all men, and every searcher for it may tell what he thinks he has found. If he is proved to be wrong, the discussion excited will help to establish the right, and his failure will be a stepping-stone in the path of progress.

Religious subjects have received the chief attention throughout my life; and I venture to state some results of my study and observation, in the hope that some who are endeavoring to preserve an inherited, but distrusted belief may be encouraged to think for themselves. Doubt is the father of knowledge, and its questionings may as rightly be applied to religion as to astronomy.

Some who do not care to read the theological and philosophical works of scholars may peruse and be helped by a simple narrative of personal experience and thought, for, as a German proverb says, "What comes from the heart goes to the heart"; and the following thoughts are the result of years of earnest, prayerful seeking after "divine truth."

A shrinking from publicity is overcome by the desire for usefulness; and the fear of unpopularity is allayed by the sentiment expressed in the words of F. A. Lange, "Never has the thoughtful observer the right to be silent, merely because he knows that for the present there are but few who listen to him."

I was born in Boston on the first day of winter, 1839. My father* often pointed out to me a spot in the corner of his study, where, when he first heard that another son had been given to him, he kneeled and commended the newly given life to God. On the first day of spring, I was "dedicated to God in baptism" at the old church in Essex Street, my father preaching a sermon from the words, "And it came to pass after the death of Abraham that God blessed his son Isaac."

My mother wrote in her journal on this day, "I

---

* Rev. Nehemiah Adams, D.D.

took a strong hold on God as a covenant God, not only mine, but my husband's and our parents' before us, even to remote generations; and I left my vow on his altar to bring up this child for him, patiently bearing any care and fatigue which in behalf of this child I may be called to endure." These vows were faithfully fulfilled, until her death from consumption when I was just eight years old. All my memories of her are pleasant, though I have but few distinct recollections of my intercourse with her. The two things which seem most forcibly stamped upon my mind are the Sunday afternoons when she talked with us and taught us the Westminster Assembly's Shorter Catechism, and the incongruous fact that on a Fourth of July she allowed me to smoke a sweet-fern cigar,—an indulgence so contrasted with the usual restraint of my life that my wonder and gratitude have vividly remained.

In her journal, she speaks of me at the age of four as having been "such a comfort and joy to us ever since he was born." I will record a few of her complimentary statements, as they are interesting illustrations of the total depravity which theoretically possessed me; and I make no other apology for quoting a fond mother's praises. She writes: "His most striking trait of character is a sense of justice. He sees things as they are, and acts accordingly in a way far different from any child I have had the opportunity of noticing." "With regard to his faults, I do not know of one that I could mention. I asked his father and aunt if they could tell me what his prominent failings were, but they neither of them could. Still, he occasionally needs my saying, 'That is naughty,' or 'That is not right,' only, when he is reminded of doing wrong, he is usually willing to do right and make reparation." It is said that I went to school cheerfully, because, as I remarked, "I wanted to please Christ." "He has great power of association of ideas, in which his strength of memory also shows itself. A word will sometimes suggest a complete set of incidents which occurred long since. He thinks, works a thing out in his own mind, but does not seem so fond of learning to read as his brother. He looks through a subject at a glance. I have been surprised that a child of so much forethought and contrivance should be so free from cunning and guile. He is fair and open as the day." Some instances of forbearance and generosity are mentioned, and this part of the record closes with saying: "His school-teacher is Mrs. Lothrop, mother of the Mary Lothrop whose little memoir is the charm of Sabbath-school readers. She said to me, 'Mrs. Adams, Robert is either early to be taken to heaven, or God is qualifying him for eminent usefulness.'" Thus, it seems I was one of the good boys, who, though they may charm "Sabbath-school readers," are not so popular with the general public of to-day as the Tom Sawyers and the bad boys, whose "diaries" would be preferred to the extended account of my youth, from which the above extracts are made.

The character of my mother's Sunday talks with her children is shown in the following entry: " It is my custom Sabbath evening to tell the three older children how I have enjoyed myself, what particular truths and passages of Scripture have interested me, and what the impression is which that day has left upon my mind, with which to enter on the busy scenes of the week. Sabbath before last, as I was thus sitting with them, I said : 'Children, this morning's sermon by Rev. Mr. Phelps, of Pine Street Church, made me feel that I ought not to rest satisfied with anything but your conversion. Parental and Sabbath-school instruction is not enough, you must be born again, as much as if you were heathens.' M. (nine years old) looked very solemn. I continued : 'Your father this afternoon preached to those who sincerely desire to be Christians. M., you think you are one of those, don't you?' 'Oh, yes, mother, I am sure I do. I pray and pray, but it don't come. Do tell me what father said.' The day had been intensely cold, and owing to slight indispositions the children had been kept at home. I told them about the sermon: one hindrance to some was the fear of what their acquaintance would think. 'Ha, mother!' said M., 'that ain't mine. I don't care what they think. Mother, I should be proud, *proud* to have them know I was a Christian.' Another hindrance was being afraid to trust the soul with Christ. 'I ain't afraid to,' she said. Another hindrance was loving one's lusts and passions. Here, we were interrupted. The next morning she said to me: 'Mother, I know what my hindrance is. I love my passions too well to give them up.'" Shortly after, it is written: " Sabbath evening M. came into my chamber, and said: 'Mother, I feel solemn, there is a weight on my mind, and I can't get rid of it.' I asked her what it was. She replied, 'It seems as if all the wicked things I have ever done against you have come into my mind to-day, and I must answer for them all at the judgment seat of Christ. They will all appear there.' Then, she mentioned several of them. She was afraid to go to bed. I went up with her. Her feelings were very solemn and tender. Conviction of sin is a new feeling for her. Oh, how I would welcome the Spirit of God, if he would but come 'under my roof'!"

A few months after this, it is said that M. printed a statement which she handed to her mother. It was headed, "Give an account of thy stewardship." After enumerating several trivial faults, exaggerated by a morbid conscience, she says: "To-day, I gave myself to God to be his child forever. I am now going, through his strength, to try not to be impudent, not to call names, and not to use any vulgar language, and not to have a coarse voice. I am not going with any of my bad companions. That little child (M. D.), ten years old, as old as I am, is a Christian; and I will try to be one too. I hope by New Year's day, at the beginning of the year, I shall be a Christian. I will read my Bible, and may I always 'consider every day as a blank leaf to be filled up for Christ.' May I always remember God will bring me to judgment. May I be a praying child, and on my dying bed may I look back with happy remembrance to this day."

The next week, my mother writes of having had to find fault with M., and says, "I told her that, in view of what she had resolved the past week, I considered it the greatest sin she had ever committed." Then follows another letter, filled with the agony of repentance and fresh resolves.

The all-overshadowing memory of my early life is this striving for conversion, which pervaded the whole family and was my own most intense idea. Being more reticent and retiring than some others of the family, I do not seem to have made as many demonstrations to my parents as they; and, therefore, I give some records of their experiences, as showing the religious atmosphere of our home and the feelings which I entertained in common with them.

My brother possessed a highly emotional nature, and was "converted" several times over. Some instances of his and my sisters' experiences will serve to illustrate my own, as I am conscious of having passed through many such strivings, though never gaining such "assurance of salvation." His first letter, written at the age of seven, is preserved. The contents were: "My dear mother, I hope that you will pray for me, that I may be one of Jesus' flock." A record of a fault and its confession says that W. came to his father, and said: "O father, last night I could not go to sleep, it worried me so; and I thought I never could be a Christian till I told you of it, and I prayed to God to forgive me, and to help tell you of it. And, father, I have felt all day like Pilgrim with a burden on his back." Though irrelevant, I will insert the next record as showing that there were limits to his Scriptural knowledge: "This morning at family worship, reading of the land of Ham in the 105th Psalm, his father asked W. what land was meant. 'The land where hams grow, father.'"

On the anniversary of our baptism, she writes: "I reminded them of it. We talked it over alone. W. was very much affected. He shed tears, and then locked himself in his chamber." We both printed verses of Scripture, which our mother pinned up on the wall of our room, "that they may be reminded of it each morning."

More than two years after my sister M.'s conversion and fall from grace already mentioned, it is said: "On this same Sabbath eve, my dear child M. came to me and said, 'Mother, I cannot but hope that I am a child of God.' I asked her why she hoped so. She replied: 'This last week, I have known what despair was. I have been in such distress about my sins. I thought, For twelve long years I have sinned against God. I asked God to forgive me my twelve long years of sin, because Christ has suffered and died for such sinners as me. I feel happy, and I want everybody to love God.' She told me a few weeks since that she had always felt entering her teens would be an important period in her life, a turning point in her history, and she meant to spend the intervening months (from April to August) in trying to become a Christian. Yesterday, W. came to his father at noon and said, 'Father, I hope that I am a Christian.' 'What makes you hope so, my son?' 'This morning, father, I felt I was a great sinner, and went to my chamber and asked to be forgiven, and gave myself to God.' He incidentally said that, at the time when he gave himself to the Lord, after he had done so, he sat down in his chamber and sang, 'Jesus, save my dying soul.'" Then comes an entry about myself when seven years old: "Sunday before last, R. said in my presence, 'I wish I was a Christian, but it's dreadful hard.' I said, 'Why, it is only to be like Christ.' Looking in my face, he asked in a deliberate, earnest manner, 'Mother, do you think you are like Christ?' Last Sunday he was sitting in my lap, and I said, 'If you could have what you wish, I know you would wish to be a Christian?' 'Well,' said he, 'I'd about as lief be a fairy.' 'Why?' 'Because then I could wish myself anything.' 'And what would be your first wish, if on waking to-morrow morning you should find yourself a fairy?' 'I would wish myself a Christian.'"

"Yesterday, W. was ten years old. This morning, Sunday, he came into his father's study, and said: 'Father, I do think I am a Christian. I believe I have taken God for my portion.'" Two months later, "W. had an affecting conversation with his father, and then followed him in prayer, beginning with, 'My sins are more in number than the sands on the sea-shore.' He afterward asked his eldest sister to pray with him, weeping freely and saying 'Oh, you don't know what a sinner I am!'"

The Calvinistic doctrine of the perseverance of saints, "once in grace always in grace," does not seem to have been impressed upon us; and, a year after this, W. experiences another conversion. My mother's hand had ceased to write her loving comments; and my father continues her journal, and says: "This morning, as I was preparing to go to meeting, W. came into my study and laid the following letter before me, and went out. To-morrow, he is eleven years old. 'My dear father, I have been led to know how vile I am, and that Jesus cleanseth from all sin; and I have cast my burden upon the Lord. I have cried unto him, and he has heard me; and the Saviour seems dear to me. I will trust in him all the days of my life. He is a good Saviour, and I will put my trust in him. My dear father, you have been the means of my loving the Saviour. You have showed me the way, I have followed it. My father, I never knew what a Saviour was. I see him nailed to the cross for me, bleeding, dying for me. Dear Saviour, how I do love thee! How I will serve thee! And, if I live to grow up, I will go far and wide and tell the poor heathen what a Saviour thou art. My father, the Lord has taken me up. I will go through my eleventh year with the Saviour. Your dear, affectionate son, W.

"'P. S.—Father, I feel the love of a Saviour.'

"He followed me into my room after meeting, and said that for a long time, when Saturday evening was coming on, he had felt a dreadful burden. The approach of holy time seemed to make him think of his sins the week past. To-day, he said, he had prayed and wept and begged for mercy in his room, and during his prayer he thought that he was heard and answered. He never felt so before, and he poured out his heart in this letter. Dear boy, he has had deep convictions of sin. So has C. This gives me confidence in whatever of right feeling they have. He said that he thought, while I was preaching the New Year's sermon this morning ('Lord, make me to know mine end'), if God had sent him word that he might die this year, and asking if he was willing to die or not, he would send back word, 'Father, thy will be done.' I am deeply interested and affected by his experience and appearance to-day."

The journal was discontinued soon after this entry, but contains an expression of my father's deep emotion at the bereavement which had befallen him in the loss of his beloved wife. The following instruction is then recorded for his children's benefit, when they should read it in later years:—

"God afflicts the soul of a child of his with these unutterable sorrows. He does not spare him. Bereavement with all its aggravating memories, its fearful solitude, its anticipations, consume him. All this happens to one who loves God.

"Now, this makes me think and feel how willing and able God is to see the wicked suffer hell torments. We have no adequate conception, till we are in great affliction, what the future sufferings of the wicked can be. 'If these things are done in the green tree, what shall be done in the dry?' 'And if the righteous scarcely be saved, where shall the ungodly and the sinner appear?' All the consolations of religion cannot prevent the memory of past joys from being unutterably painful. What must it be to lie down in sorrow! Besides, if the Saviour suffered as he did for you, and you reject him, there will be no unwillingness on the part of God to inflict torment. Constituted as we are, it is easy for God to make us completely miserable, just by withdrawing some things from us. O my dear children, flee from the wrath to come. 'It is a fearful thing to fall into the hands of the living God.' These two verses in the prophet Nahum appear to me to be exceedingly impressive: 'God is jealous, and the Lord revengeth, and is *furious:* the Lord will take vengeance on his adversaries, and he reserveth wrath for his enemies.' '*The Lord is good*, a stronghold in the day of trouble; and *he knoweth them that trust in him.*'" Sixteen years afterward, he opened the book and added some final comments, closing with the words: "My sorrows have deepened in me a conviction of future endless misery, and have helped me, I hope, to flee from the wrath to come. I am persuaded that God is able and willing to see men suffer hereafter. He can look on pain, especially when men have refused a dying Redeemer. Oh, may my children escape these things, and stand with me before the Son of Man."

These remarks and anecdotes will show the type of religion which pervaded our home, causing us periods of distressful fear of God; but, fortunately, our earthly father was love and tenderness personified, and though subject, either from temperament or creed, or both combined, to seasons of deep depression, his gloom never was manifested in harshness or willingness to see his children suffer.

II.

My brother's conversion, last recorded, was soon forgotten; and, when about sixteen years old, he became a Christian "for good," after an experience somewhat resembling those of his earlier years. He never wavered after this; but through college and his ministry, until his lamented death at the age of forty-two, he was steadfast in the faith, and through great trials exhibited a patience, forbearance and gentleness, which, joined to the strong will and ardent temperament that he possessed, caused those who knew him best to regard him as a perfect character. He held to his father's theological views in the most minute particulars, and in every sermon portrayed the terrors of eternal doom and the hope of the atonement. Though an orator of great power, his stern theology was not relished by the lax New England churches, who, though professedly holding it in their creeds, yielded inconsistently to the enlightened spirit of the age, and tried to ignore what in honesty they should disavow. One of his hearers remarked to me, while deprecating the plainness of his preaching: "We don't go back on the old doctrines; but, you know, times have changed, and—eh— You understand."

We went to church Sunday morning, and to Sunday-school and church in the afternoon; after which, the time before tea was recognized as a period for retirement and reflection. Never shall I forget the mental experiences of those hours, and my efforts in them "to become a Christian." I would read a little in Doddridge's "Rise and Progress," Allein's "Alarm," Baxter's "Saints' Rest," or some other standard book of that sort; and, having gained a certain amount of fervor, I tried to convince myself of sin by self-examination and reflection upon my "ruined state by nature,"— for, having no heinous sins of my own, I had to rely for agony upon Adam's transgression. Then, I pictured to my mind Christ's sufferings upon the cross *for me;* dwelt upon the thorns, the nails, the spear, and sought to impress my feelings till the tears flowed. Then, I thought I had gained a penitent state. I prayed in agony for forgiveness, and lingered on my knees for some evidence of conversion.

Sometimes, I felt a certain amount of peace after these exercises; but, not having such joy as I had read that others experienced, I never dared to believe that I was converted, and at frequent intervals, after I was ten years of age, these strivings were repeated.

I had some good Sunday-school teachers; but I enjoyed most the ministrations of a gentleman who, after a few minutes spent upon the regular lesson, read to us from a book about the tortures of the Spanish Inquisition. He suddenly left for the West, having forged a check; and we lost this weekly feast of horrors.

I was well grounded in the Catechism. Fox's "Book of Martyrs" and the "New England Primer" were my chief Sunday picture-books, it being wicked to look at "week-day books" on the holy day. I remember running shrieking to my father's room, thinking, in nightmare, that the skeleton with a scythe that adorns the "Primer" was after me.

Vividly do I remember the Sunday evening gatherings in the parlor after tea, when verses and hymns were recited by each in turn, and we eagerly listened to the prattling song of the youngest:—

"I love my Shepherd's voice.
His watchful eye shall keep
My wandering soul among
The thousands of his sheep.
He feeds his flock, *he calls 'em names*,
His bosom bears the ten-der lambs."

One of the earliest hymns that I recited was:—

"Welcome, welcome, dear Redeemer,
Welcome to this heart of mine."

But my great favorite was :—

"Lo! he comes, in clouds descending,
Once for favored sinners slain."

I recall saying, with broken voice and intense feeling :—

"Just as I am, without one plea."

After the hymns were said, we were asked to tell anything we had heard or thought of during the day; and, if we could muster up a quotation from a sermon or a pious reflection of our own, we were very proud. These were enjoyable seasons, but I realize now how very emotional they were. It was the climax of the day, after which the evening singing and talking, or the "monthly concert of prayer for foreign missions" at Park Street Church, where we could get into a pew with other ministers' sons, gave an agreeable reaction. The excitement was not lessened, though varied, one evening, when one of these boys swallowed the ten-cent piece destined for the collection-box.

Among my schoolmates was a boy who, in beauty of person, mental capacity and loveliness of disposition, was unrivalled in the estimation of all who knew him. I became in love with him to a degree approaching infatuation. All that pertained to him was precious to me, and his presence was bliss. I even hesitated to pray that my love to God might be increased, lest in some way that might diminish my love for Arthur.

My younger sister—ten years old—had been writing letters to her schoolmates, urging them to attend to the salvation of their souls; and, when the summer vacation separated me from my beloved friend, it occurred to me to imitate her, and make this the theme of a letter to him, asking if he did not desire to be a Christian. He replied in fervid terms, saying, "I do, I do;" and all summer a correspondence was carried on, filled with intense religious emotion. I determined to become a Christian before I met him again; and, one Sunday afternoon, I got upon my knees with the resolve to remain there till God converted me. For two hours, I wept, prayed and implored for salvation, until, tired out, I arose with the feeling that I had done my part, and, if God wouldn't do his, and save me, I must accept the fact that I was not one of the elect, and must resign myself to going to hell. I felt a peaceful satisfaction at having done my best, but had no assurance that I was a Christian.

When I met my friend in the fall, our diffidence was so great that not a word was said about our correspondence, nor was the subject of religion ever alluded to in our future conversation. This evidences the unnaturalness of such mental exercises. He was converted a few years later under the influence of a sermon, and joined the Church; but his fair and promising life was blighted by disease, and the hopes inspired by his exquisite character and uncommon powers of intellect perished in his early grave.

At the age of three, I was sent to school, probably more with a view to be kept out of the way than for regard to my intellectual needs. I can remember sitting in a little rocking-chair and learning to sew small bags for holding spools of thread; but my other lessons are not recalled, though it seems to me that I was born with the ability to read, for I do not remember ever having learned the art. At an early age, I entered the Brimmer School, then in charge of that excellent teacher, Mr. Joshua Bates, ably assisted by Mr. John H. Butler and Mr. Daniel C. Brown. I was often at the head of my classes, and devoted much time out of school to the preparation of my lessons. I can remember sitting in school with folded arms, almost bursting with self-consciousness and satisfaction at my high rank and the approval of my teachers. The studies were wisely chosen, except that

English grammar was drilled into the boys by rote before they were capable of understanding its principles, and they still talked "bad grammar" in the playground. All that I ever learned in school of history, geography, and physics was gained here; and the days when natural philosophy was taught and illustrated by experiments with apparatus were the most enjoyable days of my school life, and, I believe, the most profitable. I was removed from these useful studies before the last year of the course, in order to pursue a more classical routine. In a private school for a year I was confined almost wholly to Latin, French, and algebra, and then entered the Boston Latin School, which was under the charge of the renowned teacher, Francis Gardner. The usual course of study required five years; but Mr. Gardner announced that an "advanced division" would be formed of the best scholars, which would be put through in four years. My ambition was the only reason for joining this class, and led to my being "put through" most literally in one year. Latin and French occupied nearly the whole of our attention, but the former was the great study. Andrews and Stoddard's Latin Grammar had to be committed to memory, and was recited in this way. The first boy called upon began the lesson, then another was called at random, who must continue where the first left off. If he failed to do so accurately, it was accounted an error, and every important word missed was an error. The boys were told that, if they were conscious that they could not have recited what another boy was saying or could not have answered a question asked another, they must count an error; and, at the close of the lesson, each was asked in turn how many errors he had, and was marked accordingly. Five was the highest mark given for lessons, and each error caused a deduction of one; and, if as low a mark as two was given at any recitation, the pupil failed to receive an approbation card at the end of the week. A few conscientious boys counted errors to themselves; but others, among them some of the poorest scholars, never acknowledged errors except for public failures. Thus, a direct premium was offered for lying, where detection was impossible; and my indignation was intense at being outranked sometimes in the "placing" at the end of the month by an inferior and less truthful scholar. Being morbidly conscientious, I often turned the benefit of a doubt against myself, or else was distressed with self-accusations that I could not have recited correctly, if I had been called upon. A similar rule was adopted as to conduct. When Mr. Gardner left the room, instead of appointing a "monitor" to act as spy, he said, "I leave you upon your honor." On his return, he asked, "Who have been out of order?" The "good boys" raised their hands, and were marked for disorder; but the bad boys, who had incited all the whispering and mischief, made no sign, and took home their approbation cards to their proud parents at the end of the week, provided their public lesson failures had not forfeited them. This system of reciting made me study intensely. I could repeat the Latin Grammar verbatim from the beginning, and its list of "exceptions" will haunt me all my life. But little time was taken for play; and I often cried at being sent to bed at nine o'clock, in fear that I had not properly memorized my lesson. My friend Arthur was in this class; and his wonderful genius enabled him to stand easily first, without great effort. I one month stood first, but was usually second, except when one of the non-confessors superseded me. I approached school and recitation with fear and trembling; and, after a year of this strain, headache was fastened upon me, and, after repeated attempts to continue with my class, I was obliged to leave school, and the family physician ordered me to sea.

III.

I HAD made a voyage to Spain as a passenger, and was about to start on a voyage to England. Sea life had deadened my religious impressions somewhat; and the profanity which prevailed on shipboard had become familiar to my ear, though not to my lips. My brother and I had a small billiard-table in an upper room, upon which we had given instructions to some of the deacons' sons, to the scandal of certain good ladies of the parish. A pious and faithful servant, who had been sixteen years in the family, tossed this table out of window one night; and we rescued it, badly broken, from a neighboring yard the next day. That night, as Barbara sought her couch, her bed collapsed in ruins, and proved that "Providence" is often on the side of small boys as well as of "the heaviest artillery." Let me record here that, one spring, when the snow melted in the West Roxbury woods, old Barbara was found peacefully sleeping her last sleep, with her head upon her muff, she having strayed away in the fall in aberration of mind and laid herself down to die.

The billiard-table was repaired after a fashion, though its bed was hardly a dead level; and, during one exciting game with my brother, I startled him, and myself also, by uttering my first oath. That evening, my father called me into his study, and asked me if I did not feel that I could call myself a Christian. I answered, "No." He then asked me to write out a statement of my religious feelings which he might read to the examining committee of the church, saying that he would like to have me make some sort of an avowal before sailing upon another voyage. I did this, and accompanied him to the meeting, where my letter was read, and some of the good deacons put questions to me, which I answered; but I told them frankly I did not feel warranted to call myself a Christian. The next day, I was astounded at being told by my father that I was accepted for admission to the Church. My brother was little less than thunderstruck, for he evidently considered me less pious than I had ever been. My father said he had long believed I was a Christian, without being conscious of it myself, and that, if I would begin and endeavor to live like one, the evidences would come to me. After my voyage to England, I decided to adopt the sea as my profession; and, accordingly, I shipped before the mast in a clipper ship, bound on a voyage around the world. At my father's request, I joined the Church; and I gradually accustomed myself to the belief that I was a Christian.

I soon after entered upon life in a ship's forecastle. My surroundings were not what would be called edifying, nor would they be considered "means of grace." My church vows were a conscious restraint upon me, but neither these nor the fear of God exercised so strong a hold upon me as my father's love. He had been both father and mother to me; and my reverence and affection for him were so great that he always controlled me without commands, his usual utterances being, "I wouldn't do so," or "I think you had better not do that." Now that I was separated from him, in any temptation the first thought that came to me was, "What would my father say?" And this so governed me that, after years of roving about the world, I was able to say to him I could not recall an act that I should be ashamed to tell him.

For two years, between the ages of seventeen and nineteen, I remained on shore in a counting-room in Boston. Being thrown again into religious surroundings, and a great revival being then in progress all over the land, I began to test my evidences of conversion. I recalled the manner of my joining the Church; and, realizing that I never had anything like the ecstatic sensations which were proclaimed on all hands by new converts, I fell into despondency, and regarded myself as a false professor; feared I had committed the unpardonable sin, and grieved away the Holy Ghost; and that, in partaking of the Lord's Supper, I had eaten and drank unworthily, and had thus eaten and drank damnation to myself (I. Cor. xi., 29). For some months, gloom and despair haunted me, and I could understand why people committed suicide; but, at last, I resolved to think no more of the past, but to be a Christian from the present. A paper of Addison's in the *Spectator*, No. 465, "Means of Strengthening Faith," greatly assisted me, especially his first rule,—that, being once convinced of the truth of any article, we should never after suffer ourselves to call it in question; and my father taught me that joy and peace were not invariable accompaniments of conversion, but were blessings which God, for wise purposes, might sometimes withhold for a time. Now, I began a truly "religious life"; became a Sunday-school teacher, picking up my class from the streets and in house to house visiting; distributed tracts on the sly, dropping them on the Common or leaving them secretly on seats; made addresses at neighborhood meetings among the poor, and started a young men's prayer-meeting. The pastor and deacons disapproved of this, and thought we should exercise our gifts in the church prayer-meeting. After awhile, we yielded to their desires; and they took pains to "bring us forward." I used to crouch behind a pillar at the Friday evening prayer-meeting, dreading the words, "Brother A., will you lead in prayer?" This became a great bondage to me; and the happiest moments of the week were when the leader said, "We will close with the doxology," and I had escaped a call. All the week, I dreaded the approach of that evening, yet never failed to attend, and sometimes refused most attractive invitations, because they came on prayer-meeting night. The joyous life that many of my acquaintances led, by comparison, increased the sombreness of my own; and I recall these two years as the gloomiest period of my life.

My health obliged me to take to the sea again; and I followed it steadily for several years, working painfully through all the grades of third mate, second mate, mate, and captain. The life was always uncongenial to me, and unsuited to my disposition and tastes; but I accepted it as a providential calling, and, by faithful devotion to duty, I in a measure overcame the lack of natural aptitude.

My voyages were mostly long ones, in "deep water," as sailors say. I made short voyages to the Mediterranean and the Baltic, but California, China, the East Indies, and British India were the most frequent destinations. I sailed twice around the world, and several times half-way around, and back the same way. Seven times I sailed past Cape Horn, and ten times I passed the Cape of Good Hope. The distances sailed on the various voyages amount to about three hundred and fifty thousand miles.

For several years, I accepted implicitly the scheme of theology in which I was educated. If a question arose about any doctrine, I consulted the Catechism and the Bible; and, if the latter was not intelligible, I referred to Scott's Commentary for an explanation. What satisfied Thomas Scott's intellect I thought should be sufficient for my humble mind; but, if a final appeal became necessary,

I consulted my father's book, "Evenings with the Doctrines," and that settled the matter. Doubt was sinful, and sceptical or controversial works were to be read only by trained theologians who had been skilfully educated to combat them. The Catechism got well mixed up in my mind with the Bible and Milton's "Paradise Lost"; and a Methodist Bible-class leader at the Young Men's Christian Association, good Captain Girdler, snubbed me painfully, when I asserted, in reply to his attacks upon election, that the Bible said, God "hath foreordained whatsoever comes to pass" (using the words of the Catechism). I never had really thought for myself upon religious doctrines until my first voyage as master of a vessel, when, on an East India voyage, I visited the ports of Singapore and Penang. There, I met some English missionaries who held the doctrines of the Plymouth Brethren; though, when asked if they belonged to that sect, they answered, "Oh, *dear*, no!" I learned afterward that the Brethren had differed upon some such question as whether Christ would have sinned if he could, or could have sinned if he would; and those who held to the "peccability" of Christ were excluded from communion with the Plymouth body. A very bitter conflict arose; and any one who had not "judged the evil" was worse than a heathen to the original sect, led by John Darby. These good men first instilled dissent into my mind.

I was a strict Sabbatarian, and they startled me with the declaration that the Lord's day was in no sense the Sabbath. I believed in infant baptism; and they taught believer's baptism, with immersion as the mode. I had taken in all Scott's spiritual interpretations of the Old Testament prophecies and his theory of the Book of Revelation, which maintained that nearly all its prophecies had been fulfilled in past history, and soon the "drying up of the Euphrates"—which meant the decline of Turkey—would be followed by the millennium. But these Brethren taught the principle of the literal interpretation of the Scriptures,— that they might be read and understood without note or comment by any one who undertook the task under the guidance of the Holy Spirit. They declared that God meant what he said, and that it was a sin against the Holy Ghost to explain away the direct meaning of his words by interpreting all the promises made to the Jews as foretelling blessings to the Christian Church. This principle led to the theory that the Jews would yet be restored to Palestine, Christ would appear to the select few on earth, and they would meet him in the air with the dead saints, who would rise in the first resurrection. Then, the "marriage supper of the Lamb" would take place, and, in the mean time, antichrist would gain power over the earth; but, at the height of his persecutions of the

Jews, Christ and his followers would appear "in flaming fire, taking vengeance on them that know not God." Then, the kingdom of Christ would be established upon earth, and a thousand years of blessedness would ensue, after which, a brief and decisive conflict with Satan would follow, and the second resurrection and last judgment would end the record of this present world. They objected to the present one-man ministry of the churches, and declared that the New Testament taught the liberty of ministry of all believers, according to their gifts. They made much of the indwelling and guidance of the Holy Spirit. Their disapproval of commentators was chiefly directed toward the standard works; and they urged me to read Macintosh's "Notes," and gave me a good supply of tracts relating to their views. I studied the Bible diligently at sea, and in time came to accept many of their doctrines.

I especially saw that Jesus foretold, and the apostles believed in, his speedy return to the earth to destroy the wicked and establish his kingdom; and the system of interpretation, which made all these yearning hopes, expressed on nearly every page of the New Testament, to be merely prophetic forecasts of spiritual blessings to the "Church" two thousand years later, did violence to all my conceptions of the common-sense way of treating language. Let any one read what Paul says, "by the word of the Lord," in I. Thess. iv., 13-18, and say if the expression "*we* that are alive and remain unto the coming of the Lord," and the whole tenor of the passage, does not require the honest admission that these events were looked for during the lifetime of some then living. They were mistaken, and Paul's inspiration was disproved; but the Brethren found some ingenious excuses to save this last admission, though I now see them to be as dishonest as the theories I abandoned.

While at sea, I took much interest in the welfare of sailors. In my early experience, I saw and heard a good deal of the hardship and abuse which came to their lot, much of which seemed to me unnecessary. To improve their condition on shipboard, I studied control by moral suasion, improvement in food, and in the hours and methods of work. To enable them to overcome the temptations of life in port, I endeavored to elevate their characters by moral and religious instruction, and their minds by lectures and educational classes. Religious services were held, Bibles and tracts freely supplied, and temperance pledges obtained. The result commended all these measures to my mind. A few cases of conversion occurred; and, on one voyage, five professed "a change of heart." I wrote an account of this voyage for publication, and inserted narratives of the religious experience of the sailors. I afterward heard such reports from four out of the five that I felt obliged in honesty to withdraw these records and publish the book without allusion to them. My views about sailors will be found in "On Board the 'Rocket.'"

I found it easy to secure resolutions of moral reform, but felt disappointed in my efforts to secure "conversions." The influence during the voyage just mentioned was largely through a sailor who was converted in the first month of the outward passage, an ignorant but intensely enthusiastic man, who aroused the emotions of his shipmates. I preached "the pure gospel" over and over,—sin, eternal doom, and the atonement. But I thought often I should have succeeded better, as to the number of my converts, if I could have been more passionate and less rational. Orthodox conversion is oftener the result of feeling than of reasoning. "Religion off Soundings," a little pamphlet published by the American Seaman's Friend Society, gives my ideas about religious effort at sea.

On my East India voyages, we called, for the last port, at Padang, on the west coast of Sumatra, to fill up with coffee and cassia. The consignee, a kind and intelligent Dutch gentleman, invited me to reside with him; and often, in the evenings, we sat on the spacious veranda, stretched out in reclining chairs, in those free-and-easy attitudes which Eastern travellers will recall, and my host sometimes indulged in attacks upon the Bible representations of the Jew's Jehovah and the Christian's God, while I stoutly defended the inspired Word of God. The waving palms, the balmy air filled with delicious scents, the singing beetles, the glistening fire-flies, the tinkle of the Swiss musicbox, and the luxurious repose were suggestive of paradise; but most incongruous seemed these blasphemous attacks upon what were to me the most sacred ideas.

I found infidelity very prevalent in the Dutch settlements of Java and Sumatra, and I was told that a large number of infidel books had been scattered there some years before, and had produced a marked effect. The Lutheran minister at Padang preached orthodox sermons on Sunday, as obliged by the government under whom he held his position; but, on the week days, he told his hearers privately that he did not believe the doctrines he preached. Upon my return home, I fortified myself with tracts and books on the inspiration of the Bible, and, studying these at sea, I vigorously contended with my sceptical friends, during subsequent visits to the East India ports. I never heard that I made any converts; but, on the other hand, I got my mind impressed with many forcible arguments against the puritanical theology that I had been taught to regard as the final form of truth.

IV.

In my voyages to India and China, I was greatly impressed with the sight of the multitudes of people and their varying religions. Human life seems to be a weed that grows rankly over these lands. Its individual value appears to be small; and I was often oppressed with the questionings of my mind as to the immortality of these herds of coolies, and as to the idea that God was concerning himself separately with each one, deciding his destiny in heaven or hell. As I visited the mission rooms and saw twenty or thirty of the elect gathered out of a million heathen, it seemed incredible that these were to be saved, because, by accidental circumstances, they had come under the influence of the missionaries and been converted, and the rest of the million were to endure eternal torment. Adam's sin and their own shortcoming from the teachings of the creation had sealed their doom. These theories do not shock one so much in the prayer-meeting at home, where one sees only the elect, and the poor heathen are ten thousand miles away; but, when you see the toiling millions pass by you, and when you become acquainted with individuals and find them to be brother-men and not weeds, and observe kindly and virtuous traits of character, and witness instances of family affection and neighborly benevolence, this whole scheme of damnation excites such a feeling of revolt that only the utter extinction of one's reason and a blind acceptance of "the Word of God" can preserve one's belief. A Calvinist who wishes to keep his faith should never travel and never read secular books. By confining his acquaintance to the circle of the church and feeding his mind constantly upon evangelical reading, he may be safe. This is the life that many pietists lead; but it is so unnatural, it seems impossible that it can be right or can develop the best sort of men.

I was surprised to see the morality that prevailed in Asiatic lands. I could not observe that the people I came in contact with were any worse than the laboring and mercantile classes that a shipmaster meets in Christian lands; and, sometimes, the unwelcome conviction was forced upon me that the heathen were the best. They were infinitely the most temperate, and no more dishonest. The people who had not met with mercantile Christians were better in their habits than those who lived at the sea-ports. The seeming injustice of sending these people to hell on account of Adam's sin and their own shortcomings from the teachings of the light of nature was a weight upon my mind that I could never get rid of, though I tried to "lay my reason at the feet of Christ," as

I once heard a Boston lady in spectacles say at a "holiness" meeting.

When I first visited China, I was told by the missionaries at Fuh Chau that they had just baptized the first convert to Christianity after eleven years of labor in a district containing three million people. It occurred to my mind that God had not devised very effective machinery for "making disciples of all nations"; and I recalled the enthusiasm at home in the monthly concert of prayer for foreign missions, when a letter from a missionary told of a few conversions, and how the leader of the meeting would give out the hymn,—

"The morning light is breaking,
The darkness disappears,"—

which would be sung with great fervor.

On the spot, the conversions only excited a painful comparison.

My father was for thirty-six years a member of the Prudential Committee of the American Board of Commissioners for Foreign Missions, and was devoted to their work. In his later years, I took him on a voyage around the world in the ship "Golden Fleece." At Canton, he visited the missions he had been so accustomed to delight in; and, when he saw the result of all these years of effort and contrasted it with the vast, surging tide of heathenism that rolled around him, he was greatly depressed, and said to me, "I don't believe the world will ever be converted by the preaching of the gospel."

These impressions never made me disparage missionary effort; for I believed it did some good, and was necessary to Christian consistency. It only excited wonder at God's way of doing things. How an omnipotent and benevolent God should fail to spread his "glad tidings of great joy" to all people in an effective way was beyond my comprehension. He evidently had miraculous power enough, and had exercised it on very trivial occasions in the past. Did he not make iron swim to recover an axe? Did he not destroy two companies of fifty men with fire from heaven, because their captains did not invite Elijah in a respectful manner to "come down"? Did he not send two bears to tear forty-two children who had called names in the street? Did he not make the sun and moon stand still until the people had avenged themselves upon their enemies? If he could do such things for mere wonder or revenge, why should not love call forth his power, when countless myriads of heathen are going down to everlasting perdition for lack of a revelation they can understand? All this confounded and oppressed me, and I found no peace save in unquestioning submission and refusal to think.

In later voyages to the East Indies, I found that the Holy Ghost was leading the good "Brethren" to differ among themselves, some becoming so exclusive in their separation from evil that they could only recognize the true Church of God as existing in their own gatherings. An adventurer came to Singapore, announcing that the Holy Ghost was gathering the Lord's people to await his coming at the town of Wellington in South Africa, where all the prophecies of blessing were being fulfilled. He assembled a few brethren and sisters in a room; and, after hours of intense prayer, some were seized with an ecstasy which was called receiving the Holy Ghost. One of the sisters was prevailed upon to go to South Africa, and she wrote back letters enthusiastically declaring that "the half had not been told her." I afterward met in China a captain in the British army, who, under the influence of this man, gave up his commission, and prepared to go to South Africa. But, at Singapore, he learned that the man's lady travelling-companion was not his wife, he having left that person behind when he became "the Lord's freeman." This opened the captain's eyes; and, declaring that the Lord did not countenance debauchery, he changed his plans, greatly shaken up in mind.

Arriving in San Francisco after a passage around Cape Horn of nearly five months, in which I had attained to a great degree of faith and consecration through constant study of the Bible and the literature of the Brethren, I experienced a great shock from the words and demeanor of the ministers and Christians of that city. I went to hear nine preachers while there; and none of them showed any knowledge of the Christian's calling out of the world, and none of them preached salvation by Christ. I wrote in my journal: "Ear-tickling and soul-lulling orations about benevolence, moral duties, or Scripture history, formed the sermons; and, if any direction was given to sinners, it was such as Moses preached before the righteousness of God without the law had been manifested. Nor did I meet with any warm-hearted Christians. All seemed to think more of dress, amusement, Pacific railroad and China steamers than of their Lord. It seemed impossible, from the words and attitudes of all these, that we were instructed to 'love not the world, neither the things that are in the world,' and to watch for our Lord's coming; for no one seemed to act upon such an idea, and yet they read their Bibles or studied theology continually." I could not answer this fact by the Brethren's sweeping condemnation of all believers but themselves; and, having seen their own variance of opinion, it appeared that the infallible guide, the Holy Spirit, led each prayerful believer to distinct and differing views, often utterly opposing those of other equally devout and prayerful believers. My mind was not satisfied by the theory that these views of truth were like different views of a mountain from various points of observation, and were capable of union into a harmonious whole, when seen from God's standpoint. The only solution of the differences among Christians and of the ever-varying religions and views which I found to prevail all over the world appeared to my mind to be that every man makes his own religion in accordance with his surroundings and the constitution of his mind.

A friend had presented me with Herbert Spencer's book, "Illustrations of Universal Progress." I had glanced at it and laid it aside; for I had never in my life read a book opposed to Orthodoxy, and I had understood he was one of the vain men, who, by "oppositions of science, falsely so called," were striving to make the word of God of none effect. But, about this time, I took it up, and found that its theories about religion agreed with my observation and experience. He applied the law of evolution to religion, commencing with the savage's worship of his dead chief, which developed into the conception of a deity, who, at first human in all things, has been gradually losing human likeness, each race of men forming ideas of God in accordance with their own intelligence and desires. He says, "As humanity is a growth and not a manufacture, men's theologies must be determined into such forms as the conditions require"; and it follows " that the religious creeds through which mankind successively pass are, during the eras in which they are severally held, the best that could be held." The human origin of all religion thus seemed to explain all my difficulties.

I sailed for the west coast of Mexico, and experienced a reaction from the fervor which had characterized my thoughts on the outward passage. I subsided into an indifference about religious truth, which, during two months' stay on the lonely coast of Mexico, degenerated still further into doubts concerning the whole scheme of Christian theology. I thought Satan was let loose upon me; for every form of infidelity came flooding upon my mind, and I could not read a chapter in the Bible without rationalistic suggestions of its improbability or overestimated import. I still kept up services with my sailors, though I preached what was not very authoritative to my own mind. I hope preachers on shore never do this. I remember walking off into the *monte*, as the Mexicans call the wild-brush-covered plains, and in the evening twilight I stretched out my arms to heaven, and with intense feeling called on God to reveal himself to me, and convince me of the truth of what claimed to be his written word. But no answer came. Some weeks after, when sailing toward Cape Horn, my emotions were strongly aroused by one of those trade-wind sunsets, which only voyagers know, whose glories the ablest pens would fail to describe. Suddenly, the words came to me, " Now is Christ risen from the dead." I started at the seeming lack of connection with my thoughts, and said: " Is it true? If so, the teachings of Christ and his apostles are true. I can believe anything, if that fact is established." I searched the Scriptures, aided by Scott's and Lange's Commentaries and Gilbert West's treatise on the Resurrection; and my faith increased. I made no critical study of the text for myself, but read the conclusions of these critics. The story seemed well vouched for; and, in the course of my daily study of the Greek Testament, I came upon Paul's charge to Timothy, " Remember Jesus Christ risen from the dead," implying that this was the foundation of the Christian faith. As such I resolved to receive it, and I determined to doubt no more.

I read Paul's warning to Timothy, " that in the last days perilous times shall come," "that some shall depart from the faith, giving heed to seducing spirits and doctrines of devils"; and, in his Epistle to the Thessalonians, I read, " God shall send them strong delusion, that they should believe a lie." So I tried to believe that all these logical conclusions and most reasonable ideas that seemed so to agree with my observation and common sense were only delusions characteristic of the last time, and proved that the Lord was truly at hand. So firm a hold had my Bible taken of me that reason was doomed to a still longer subjection to a blind faith, and for years all the light of science and the wisdom of the age were rejected as delusions it was dangerous and sinful to encounter.

I thought my feeling of consecration might be increased if I went through the form of believers' baptism; and, after the end of the voyage, I was immersed, one cool October day, in a New Jersey lake, by Mr. James Inglis, editor of the *Witness*, a monthly paper devoted to the truths of Brethrenism minus its exclusiveness, though Mr. Inglis had, like most of the Brethren whom I have known, gradually withdrawn from fellowship with others, and was accustomed "to break bread" on the Lord's Day in his own house with any friends who chanced to come. After the plunge, he kept me standing dripping on the shore, while he made a gospel address to the dozen stragglers who attended us. I never had placed any stress upon the mode of baptism; but I imbibed a strong opinion of the unseemliness of this mode, and ever after doubted if immersion had been divinely prescribed for all climes and periods, though I believed that baptism was only to be used as the sign of the faith of its recipient. I may add that I read books in favor of infant baptism, but nothing on the other side except the Bible. No increase of "holiness" came to me; but, by resolutely refusing to reason and keeping my sympathies warm in religious work, I kept on for years sincerely leading a Chistian life. I saw that many wise and learned men were able to accept Christianity in spite of the light of modern science, and I clung to their faith as an argument for the maintenance of my own.

V.

AFTER fifteen years of sea life, I settled down to business on shore, establishing myself in Montreal. A perusal of "Theodore Parker's Experience as a Minister" at this time, let loose my reason and aroused the old doubtings. My father had obtained the book to assist him in writing a controversial article against Parker's views, but the book rendered an opposite service to his son. Two words had a great effect upon me. He spoke of Moses as a "Hebrew filibuster." I was shocked at his irreverence in thus speaking of the man of God; but, on reflection, I asked, Why did the inroad of the Hebrews upon Canaan differ in principle from the attacks of the American filibusters upon Cuba and Mexico? It opened up a natural view of the Hebrew wars, and brought the Bible down to a common-sense interpretation. For a year, I was in great danger of an abandonment of faith, and rationalistic suggestions often crowded upon my mind.

The delight of a home, after all my wanderings, was intensely enjoyed; and I developed some love for this world and coolness toward the next, which led a good evangelist to warn me that "God would stir up my nest," if I took too much comfort in it. Having made church connections, I soon got to work again in "the Lord's vineyard," became superintendent of a Sunday-school, preached at a mission chapel Sunday evenings, and through the week took part in prayer and temperance meetings, and worked to provide for the maintenance of a sailors' institute. All this, besides an engrossing business, carried on "for Christ," left me no time for reading, reflection, or conversation, except in the line of my religious and business duties.

God "stirred up my nest" most effectually with severe afflictions, though I could not see that they were judgments, unless it was for being too religious, as some of the trials were directly traceable to my pious efforts. If I ever took a vacation or stopped to think, my reason began to attack my theology; and my only escape was to plunge back into the old career, and resolve never to doubt. My Christian friends now assure me these afflictions were "the loving chastisement of the Lord," on account of "the incipient stages of what has now become open rebellion against the Almighty."

A business visit to Europe broke up this mind burial and let loose my reason again, and it never was subdued afterward. I recall a decided mental experience at Hamburg. One Sunday morning, I attended a Lutheran church; and its candles and papist forms of worship illustrated another of the innumerable interpretations by God's people of "God's revealed will." In the afternoon, I visited the Zoological Gardens, which were thronged by respectable, orderly people with their families, who studied the rare animals and various interesting and instructive collections, listened to good music, and partook of refreshments. All this was wicked to Puritanism, but it seemed good to common-sense that the working man's day of leisure should be employed in such a manner. Why it could be better to stay at home and read how God slaughtered the Canaanites; how Jael murdered her confiding guest Sisera, and was declared "blessed above women" for it; or study the order of the service of the Jewish tabernacle,—was a puzzle. I recalled that some Christians kept the Jewish Sabbath still,—ate cold dinners, shaved on Saturday, and kept quiet all Sunday except when "walking decently to and from the house of God," as the "blue laws" express it.

Others believed the Sabbath was abrogated by Christ; and the Lord's day, a day of worship and religious joy, had taken its place. Paul said he was afraid of people who observed Sabbaths, and some Christians regard the day wholly in a spiritual light. Some observe Saturday, and others Sunday. And here on the Continent were other Christians deliberately breaking the fourth commandment and desecrating the Sabbath, according to our notions of God's law. The confusion of ideas about the day, its origin, its object, the authority for its change from Saturday to Sunday, impressed me anew with the uncertain nature of God's revelation; and why a God of intelligence could not speak plainly on such a point was past comprehension. The superior benefit to man from this feature of man's way of observing the day in Germany over "God's way" in New England was too evident to reason to be denied; and the whole history of the day through the ages, from all that I could learn by a careful study of Christian writers, only enforced the idea that men in each age had made their own ideas to be God's law. From that day, the conviction never slumbered, though sometimes somewhat suppressed.

The strain of this combined religious and business life proved unfavorable to health, and three years were passed in travel or residence with my family in other cities for the purpose of recuperation. Observation of different nations in Europe supplied fresh illustrations of the great diversity of religious opinions, and the uniform standard of morality and demeanor among all people. In thrift, neatness, courtesy, and good behavior, the inhabitants of Catholic and "infidel" France were, to say the least, not inferior to those of Protestant England and Scotland; nor did free-thinking Holland and Germany appear to disadvantage in comparison with Calvinistic Switzerland. An investigation into the various "isms" for which Boston is noted showed numbers of equally good and earnest people engaged in propagating varying views of what to each one was "God's truth." The claim of any one of these differing sects to be the divinely inspired custodians of revelation, while all others were more or less deceived in their equally confident opinions, appeared to me to be a combination of arrogance and ignorance; and my reverence for the idea of a Supreme Being compelled me to believe that, if he undertook to make a revelation, good, intelligent people would understand it alike.

On board a steamer returning from England, I came across Paine's "Age of Reason." I had avoided reading this or any other sceptical book while my mind was unsettled; but, now that my convictions were clearer as to the human origin of "revelation," I ventured to read it. My astonishment at its lofty sentiment, religious aspiration, and pure morality was intense; for was not this "the worst of books"? Its coarseness consisted in ridiculing what was indecent, immoral, and absurd in the Bible; and its logic and demonstration seemed to my mind unanswerable. Modern scholarship has cleared up a few points among the mass of matter that he criticizes; but his book still exists as a convincing demonstration that the Bible is composed of human ideas, and not of the words of God. As Paine's writings cannot be overthrown by learning and reason, scorn and calumny are used as the only remaining weapons. Let each read it for himself. If the Bible is the word of God, it need not fear the criticism of Paine. Criticisms and reviews of all other literature are deemed valuable in proportion to their exposure of defects and falsity, but with the Bible only adulatory criticism is tolerated.

Paine treats the Bible as all books should be treated by common-sense people in an age of reason; and the word of God certainly should be able to bear such examination. But his criticism proves it to be the word of man. I soon after bought a copy, and procured from the American Tract Society Bishop Watson's "Reply to Paine," said to be a perfect refutation of this attack upon the inspiration of the Bible. I read these two books chapter by chapter alternately, and tried to weigh the arguments fairly. Paine's keen, logical analysis, couched in the most lucid and forcible English, was proof against the Bishop's pompous denunciation and stale argument.

After my return to America, I spent a year in the neighborhood of Boston, and devoted myself to reading the thought of the day, especially what related to the genuineness and authenticity of the Bible, the laws of evolution and political economy, and some social problems.

The proofs of the theory of development, as portrayed in the writings of Darwin, Haeckel, and Spencer, seemed in the main to be unanswerable; and I found that almost every scientist in the world had in a great measure accepted the evolution theory. I paid great respect to the opinions of the eminent exception that exists in Montreal, to whose character and ability we all do honor, and of whom, as citizens, we are justly proud. But his objections did not satisfy me, and were overborne by the overwhelming testimony of the great scholars who have left him almost alone to the support of the theories of the past.

I therefore found a scientific foundation for my doubts about revelation; and, in the words of John Fiske, I came to believe in "divine action through natural law, instead of in divine action through supernatural fiat." The Book of Genesis and its creation stories I found to be disproved beyond any possibility of reconciliation, and I could only regard it as the record of Hebrew guesses about nature. The truth of the unfailing succession of cause and effect overthrew all possibility of miracle; and I found it easier to believe in the fallibility of the Bible writers, both of the Old and New Testaments, than in the violation of the order of nature.

The theories of evolution gave me a reasonable conception of the universe, and seemed to put solid ground under my feet. But for their disproof of supernaturalism, I might not have succeeded in shaking off the thraldom of tradition, so strong was the bond of educational and social influences that held me. Every motive of self-interest in life held me to Orthodoxy, and only what seemed to me absolute proof of its falsity could have led me to renounce its connection and associations. The path of worldly advancement now lies through the church. My good father said to me on the eve of my departure for Montreal, " I do not think we should be religious for the sake of gain, but I believe there is no surer means of advancement than to be a reputable member of a respectable church." I found it popular to be a Christian, and experience convinces me that it is he, who conscientiously leaves the church, who knows what it is to "take up the cross and follow Jesus."

It would be tedious to dwell upon the varied proofs, furnished by evolution, of the orderly development of matter and mind through past ages, without interference from either God or devil; and I presume it is unnecessary to do so, for the highest authorities tell us that every learned man in the world, who is not hampered by conventional theological ties, has accepted the theory of evolution.

Nor can I enlarge upon my consideration of the deep questions of the existence of evil, God's sovereignty and man's free agency, and all the range of Calvinistic dogma. Day by day, I pondered upon these themes; but it is difficult to tell the mental experiences of years in a few pages.

I studied the history of other religions and the character of their sacred books; and I found Christianity to be the natural development out of the dogmas and traditions of India, Persia, Egypt, Palestine, and Greece, just one step, and a great step, in advance on the path of human progress, but destined to lead to the step of the religion of evolution and still onward.

I found all the great doctrines of Christianity, such as trinity, miraculous conception, atonement and resurrection, paralleled or foreshadowed in the beliefs of many lands.

But I resolved to take my stand upon the doctrine of the resurrection of Jesus, as I had done once before, but not to read it in commentaries this time ; for this is the foundation stone of the Christian religion.

I wrote out in parallel columns all the testimonies of evangelists and apostles to the resurrection and ascension, and compared each division minutely. I advise others to do this, and judge for themselves. " God's Word " should be able to tell its own story and produce conviction.

To my mind, this story bears all the marks which characterize human legends ; and the discrepancies are such that it is impossible to believe that the vital truth of the Christian religion would not have been more impressively stated, if God undertook to reveal it to a world that would perish without it. There is a great array of literature on this subject, if any wish to read human opinions about it. I found also that contemporary history was utterly silent about this marvellous event, and even about the existence of such a man as Jesus.

As I have said, I took great interest in foreign missions during my voyages to Asia ; and it seemed unaccountable why God, who wishes all men to come to the knowledge of the truth, should have himself created the principal obstacle to their doing so. The chief difficulty in spreading ideas among heathen nations has been their varying languages. The missionary or teacher has had to spend a lifetime in learning a new language, inventing an alphabet, reducing words to writing, and translating the word of God, as nearly as his ingenuity will enable him to express involved ideas, where no words exist which can convey the sense God has revealed to English-speaking people through several other languages. Meantime, another generation has perished, while the saving truth has been in preparation.

The Bible tells us that God got angry with a few men in the land of Shinar, who were trying to build a tower that would reach to heaven. God was evidently alarmed, and said, "Now, nothing will be restrained from them, which they have imagined to do." So "the Lord did there confound the language of all the earth." He all the time was "not willing any should perish," and had "foreordained" all that should come to pass, or at least knew what would happen. He intended that the gospel should be preached to all men under heaven; and yet, for fear that some men would climb into heaven by means of a brick wall, he destroyed the universal language, and interposed the greatest possible hindrance to the spread of the truth. In order to embarrass these bricklayers, he left millions of heathen to perish, caused countless wars, and delayed the civilization and enlightenment of the world for ages, by preventing men from understanding one another. A good God would not have done this. A wise God would not have given himself such a bad character; and an intelligent God would not have feared that men could build "unto heaven," and jump off into it while the earth was revolving so swiftly on its axis. I perceived this story to be the myth of an ignorant people.

VI.

I COULD fill volumes with the record of my study and questioning about Bible doctrines. I had believed that a Christian should be a man of one book. I enjoyed a great deal of leisure when in command of vessels upon long voyages, and my tastes were almost entirely literary. This conviction of the paramount importance of religion led me to concentrate all my reading upon the Bible and theological books. I procured Lange's Commentaries as they were published, and read several of the volumes from beginning to end. One voyage was devoted chiefly to the study of the Greek Testament. I look back with regret upon these years, which, if devoted to the study of the facts of nature, would have made me a learned man; but, instead of this, I was trying to discover the probable course of future events by comparing the obscure rhapsodies of Hebrew prophets and poets, or in trying to learn the mind of God by studying the fragmentary remains of the writings of barbarous, or less enlightened ages than the present. I will not call it wasted time, because it has in the end taught me that the Hebrew Scriptures are to be judged by the same rules as the literature of all other nations, and that they possess no authority beyond what pertains to all other writings of men. I hope I may prove further that this time has not been wasted, by persuading some that it is useless to study the Bible in the hope of discovering how the world was made, or when and how it will end; when Jesus will return to earth; how the ten kingdoms of the Roman Empire are to be restored in Europe; who is to be the antichrist; or, if it be true that the British nation represents the lost ten tribes of Israel, to determine whether it will possess Constantinople, or what its future is to be. As a venerable book, the best thought of the ancients, the record of the customs and characters of men of other days, the Bible stands peerless in its own sphere, and will always be prized. It is only injured and degraded by the effort to elevate it to a sphere where it has no place.

It may be of interest to mention that my knowledge of sceptical objections to the Bible was first gained from orthodox commentaries, for I never read a sceptical work until long after my doubts had arisen. In searching Lange's Commentaries for explanations of the contradictions and obscurities of "God's Word," I often came upon refutations of the German critics, and sometimes the superiority of their opinions was strongly apparent to me. Attacks upon "heresy" thus often help to spread it; for they make known its nature, and, as "truth is mighty and must prevail," it only needs to be known to win its way. All criticism should be welcome for this reason.

The inconsistencies of Christians, myself included, led me to doubt if any really believed the doctrines they professed. Christ taught his followers not to lay up treasures upon earth, to sell all they had and give to the poor. He said the rich should hardly enter into the kingdom of heaven. The early Christians believed him, and had all things common; and Ananias and Sapphira were killed for hypocrisy in the matter. Now, Christians are foremost in the struggle for riches. They explain away the meaning Jesus evidently attached to his words and the literal sense in which his disciples understood them, and say that only inordinate affection for money is condemned; and no Christian millionaire ever believes himself guilty of that sin. They give away driblets of their incomes, for which they receive great praise, and hoard up and increase their principal. I do not say it is wrong to do this, but that it is unchristian. An old bachelor, an elder in a Presbyterian church, who had been lauded for his benevolence, lately died; and his estate footed up two millions of dollars. He had given away part of his income yearly, and once about fifty thousand dollars of his principal to found an asylum bearing his name. But in what sense had he followed Christ's teachings? Many excuse themselves in the race for gold by saying they are seeking it to do good with, to use it for Christ; but it is generally used first to do good to themselves, and supply summer and winter palaces and carriages, and to amass a capital.

Paul directs that "women adorn themselves in modest apparel with shamefastness and sobriety, not with braided hair, and gold or pearls or costly raiment"; but the wife and daughters of the Christian millionaire enter the handsome sanctuary, which has succeeded to the "upper room" of the disciples, wearing glove-fitting dresses of expensive fabric, braided hair purchased of poorer women, barbaric ear-rings and gold bracelets, and many accessories of costly raiment. I do not say that this is wrong, but is it consistent in those who believe the apostle's words to be divinely inspired?

Christians, as a rule, do not give to those that ask of them, and are apt to turn away from borrowers. They do not turn the other cheek to the smiter, nor refrain from going to law with brethren,—and that before unbelievers; and, when the plaintiff is awarded the coat, I never heard that the Christian defendant offered his "cloke" also.

The love of enemies, avoidance of public prayer, concealed alms, no anxiety for the morrow, are maxims which a few follow in intention, but which the multitude of believers wholly disregard.

The explanation given is that these things were good for the time when they were prescribed; but times have changed, and the spirit, not the letter, is to be observed. If the spirit is truly regarded, this is a satisfactory answer, provided Jesus and Paul were merely reformers of their own age; but, it is professed, these divinely inspired maxims were given by the Christ of God and the Holy Ghost through the apostle to the Gentiles for all time. If so, they are as binding to-day as when they were uttered. The Bible becomes intelligible and useful, when we see it to be men's best thoughts for the good of the times they lived in; but, when it is made out to be God's universal prescription for men in all ages, and the only compendium of infallible truth, it is as hard to accept it as such as it would be for the medical profession now to receive the works of the surgeon barbers of the Middle Ages as standards for the regulation of their practice.

Prof. Huxley, in "Lay Sermons," gives Descartes' golden rule: "Give unqualified assent to no propositions but those the truth of which is so clear and distinct that they cannot be doubted." The adoption of this rule will overthrow nearly all dogmatic theology, and it will likewise deter the inquirer from too confident an assumption of the mere *hypotheses* of evolution and the science of the day. The main conclusions which I have reached rest upon a common-sense interpretation of the facts which nature and man present to every eye. Once accept the idea that religion is the record of the aspirations of the human mind and changes from age to age and day to day, as men's capacities and natures alter, there being no infallible revelation from God of one true religion, and it will be found that all the history of human thought is intelligible. Religion, which is now to each man the blind acceptance of incomprehensible ideas, becomes a simple and common-sense affair. Instead of searching the Bible with the Holy Spirit, or swallowing whole the decisions of fathers, councils, and commentators, or surrendering one's mind to the control of ministers and priests, each man may learn for himself from the book of nature all the grand outlines of truth that are necessary to be known as general principles; and the details can be learned from the investigation of live facts by living men, instead of from musty researches by scholars among the obscure and doubtful records made by erring men in dead languages, in dark ages.

Only he who has experienced it can understand the relief that comes to the mind of one who for years has struggled to understand "the Word of God" and its complicated theology for himself, instead of taking it all for granted because his parents believed it, when at last he puts it in its right place, as records of past thought, and comes into the freedom and light of the religion of nature and humanity. He then learns that all events move in the channel of law, that these laws are ever tending in their ultimate results toward the development of good, that good and evil teach their own lessons and alike "work together for good."

The origin of scepticism in my mind was the observation of the differing and sometimes opposing views of Christians, who were studying the Bible prayerfully under the guidance of the Holy Spirit. To avoid the fatal conclusion of the human origin of their religion, which this premise leads to, Christians are accustomed to claim that the differences are upon "non-essentials," and that upon all vital points true Christians agree. They emphasize the word "true," and it means that those who think as they do are the only *true* Christians. The doctrines of the atonement and the deity of Christ they admit to be vital; but, when such godly, prayerful men as Channing and Ezra S. Gannet, with the latter of whom my father engaged in controversy upon these points, find themselves led by study of the Scriptures to the renunciation of these dogmas, they assert that these praying men have abandoned the teaching of the Spirit, each being "vainly puffed up by his fleshly mind." As the Spirit's influence is not a visible or tangible thing, and therefore cannot be demonstrated, there is no arguing with people who assert that all people who are led by the Spirit of God believe as they do, and all who differ from them have forsaken the Spirit's leading for "the vagaries of reason." When an orthodox theologian like Bushnell nearly approaches the Unitarian denial of the vicarious atonement, it furnishes an opportunity for these analyst theologians, with their hair-turning scales, to determine how many grains of ideas are the product of the Spirit and how many are from "the fleshly mind." When one praying searcher of Scripture finds sprinkling, another immersion, and another spiritual influence to be baptism, as this is "not essential to salvation," Christians excuse Jesus for not keeping his promise, "When he, the Spirit of Truth, is come, he shall guide you into all the truth,"—as though any real truth is "unessential," or any error not injurious. One finds in the Bible infant baptism, another believer's baptism; one ordination, another liberty of ministry; one a post-millennial advent, another a pre-millennial advent (a thousand years is of small account in theology); one trinity, another unity; one a personal devil, another an evil influence; one election, another free grace; one perseverance, another falling from grace; one progressive sanctification, another instantaneous sanctification; one eternal punishment, another annihilation, and another universal restoration; one an intermediate state after death, another an immediate heaven; and so on.

All these views are confidently proved from the words of the Bible by each divinely illuminated student; and each inspired believer through the ages has denounced or cursed or murdered the other inspired believer, as Calvin caused the death of Servetus for views now widely held by good men. What wars and atrocities have been caused by this curious method of the Spirit of leading Jesus' followers into all truth! (Read "The Crimes and Cruelties of Christianity," by B. F. Underwood.) And Christians dare tell us they all agree in essentials! These truths may not be essential to the salvation of the soul; but, in the past, they have been very necessary to the existence of the body. They reduce essentials finally to one dogma, salvation by Christ; and, if any one disbelieves that, it only proves he has refused to be guided by the Spirit, being "vainly puffed up by his fleshly mind." Can the human mind cease to be hindered in its advancement, till the shackles of such illogical, arrogant, and uncharitable assumptions are destroyed?

I am told it is disrespectful to my father to differ from his views, and filial reverence should keep me from proclaiming opposed ideas. What progress would the world have made, if this notion had always prevailed? Look at China's progress in knowledge. Ancestral worship has hindered advancement there. My grandfather was a worthy cabinet-maker in Salem. He decided that his son should be educated in the ideas of a certain theological sect. It is really irreverence to my grandfather that I am guilty of. A previous grandfather probably believed in hanging the Salem witches; and I am certainly irreverent to that one, and am not ashamed of it. One comfort is that, if our deceased friends are in a conscious state, they thoroughly approve of any progress we make in truth in advance of their notions. It would be a pity to find we had been grieving them, because we refused to accept the advance in knowledge since their day, or declined to use the electric light because they read by tallow candles or the light of the fire, as my father did, when a boy, for economy's sake.

Respect for my father requires me to be loyal to the truth as I see it. He never flinched in the maintenance of the facts that hell and slavery are Bible doctrines. They are taught there, and he was consistent. The leading Liberals and Abolitionists gave up the Bible, and then opposed hell and slavery; and they were consistent. But the mass of orthodox clergymen have quietly ignored hell and violently attacked slavery, and they are inconsistent. If the Bible teaches ideas opposed to reason and morals, if it is the infallible word of God, we must be unreasonable and immoral; but all difficulty is cleared away, when we see that not only common sense, but an overwhelming mass of scientific and literary criticism, proves the Bible to be the record of human thought about God. One who sees this and fears to raise his voice against a superstition which he believes to be dishonoring to God and injurious to man, he alone is false to the heritage of an honored name.

During the year that I was in Boston, I endeavored to keep my opinions to myself; for I desired not to give offence, and wished to verify my position. But watchful friends discovered that I had been a few times to a Unitarian church, that I read the Boston *Sunday Herald*, and that I entertained some doubts about the accuracy of the Mosaic story of creation. These dreadful sins brought upon me such remonstrances and exhortations that I was at last compelled to declare my true position in a letter to my friends, which I afterward decided to publish over my initials, as an easy way of informing acquaintances of my change, not supposing it would attract public attention. I had no desire to force my ideas upon them; but, for my own peace of mind, it became necessary for me to avow myself. I constantly met people who treated me with great courtesy on account of my reputation as a Christian. Some of these were friends of my father,—ministers and gentlemen whom I highly honor and esteem. After such interviews, I had so painful a sense of sailing under false colors that I preferred to incur what would seem to me undeserved blame rather than receive what I felt to be unmerited praise.

From the foregoing sketch of my religious experiences, it will be seen that my course was first to find the literal teaching of the Bible and reject the sophistries by which theologians of the present day try to make its teaching harmonize with modern ideas. I saw that, treated honestly, the Bible taught a six days' creation, the fall of man, a universal flood, an eternal hell, a vicarious atonement, and the future return of Christ to the earth. But I found Christians all at variance about these doctrines, unable to agree as to what the revelation of God really revealed. I found that many scholars doubted the genuineness and authenticity of the Gospels, and all the probabilities seemed to me to be on their side. The Dutch school of criticism gave a satisfactory explanation of the Bible as a compilation of Hebrew literature. Science, humanity and reason were opposed to tradition; and I gave up tradition. Honesty and sincerity obliged me to withdraw from membership in the Christian Church.

VII.

CONCLUSION.

A THOUGHTFUL friend advised me not to publish the foregoing statement of my experience in thought until three years had elapsed, to allow time for consideration and possibly for modification of views, which might be found to be extreme, a natural reaction from an intense and unnatural pietism. I felt this to be wise and prudent. This time has nearly passed, but reperusal suggests no alteration; and experience and reflection confirm the convictions expressed.

During this period, a great many letters have come to me; and numbers of friends, each in his own estimation led by the Spirit and holding the correct views of religious truth, have endeavored to convince me of error. I find, however, that they all differ; and to adopt the degree of supernaturalism which any one holds would still leave me at variance with the majority. I have been able to classify my correspondents into nine classes, each showing an upward step toward rationalism, and the whole forming an admirable demonstration of my assertions as to the human origin of religion. Each follows knowledge as far as his environment will allow, and then holds to "faith." Each minister, in the light of modern science, walks up to his denominational fence, and there stops; but the Congregationalist goes beyond the Plymouth Brother, the Episcopalian distances the Congregationalist, and the Unitarian ventures still nearer to rationalism. For any one to go further would subject him to trouble; and the impression made upon my own mind is that their progress is deterred by the unconscious influence of self-interest, and they demonstrate the fact that ultimate truth lies in the direction toward which each has advanced,—that is, in *Naturalism*. The person nearest to agreement with me is the most travelled of all, the one next to him is the most scientific, and next to him comes the most scholarly; then come the business men; then orthodox ministers; and the farthest off from me and the nearest to supernaturalism are emotional ladies and men who believe in the verbal inspiration and literal meaning of the Bible, and who seldom read anything else.

This gradation of opinion, and the capacities and circumstances of its exponents, strongly convince me that my future path trends forward, and not backward. In the rational study of nature lie the secrets of knowledge, and every admission of the existence of supernatural influences is a barrier to progress.

A Christian asked me, "What have you to live for now?" His tone implied that the loss of a belief in hell removed all impetus to benevolence and philanthropy. I replied: "A thousand-fold more than ever. To benefit men here and now, to promote commerce, to advance society, to influence the future of the race. The world has opened out before me full of possibility and hope, tempting me to effort by its opportunities and affording joy in its prospects. All this is gained in exchange for distressing efforts to save a few men, through emotional experiences, from an imagined impending doom, in the face of which all attempts at worldly improvement would be a hopeless and heartless mockery." It is the consistent Christian who has nothing to live for. Death or the coming of the Lord is his only hope. To depart and be with Jesus is his desired destiny. The more sincere a Christian a man is, the less has he to live for in this world; and the reason that Christianity does so little harm is because it is so little believed. The Dark Ages were the ages of "faith." The religion of nature is what most men practise, and they only espouse Christianity when it is attacked. Practically, but few believe its dogmas; and, when men are no longer paid to preach them and self-interest does not enforce conformity, they will be abandoned in name, as they are already, to a great extent, in fact.

Men have become accustomed to think that Christianity means goodness, whereas all that we prize as good existed and was recognized in the world long before Jesus was born. Orthodox Christianity means the theory that men are all doomed to eternal torment, and can only escape by belief in the merits of the death of a man-god. This creed is fast being relegated to the domain of cast-off superstitions, which have had their day and done their work in the development of those who created them. He who leaves it does not leave faith behind; but he travels in faith to a belief in the inviolable order of nature, the sequence of cause and effect, the reign of law, the upward destiny of the human race,—to faith in *good*.

A RADICAL AVOWAL.

A LETTER TO ORTHODOX FRIENDS.

You have remarked upon evidences that I was changing in my religious belief; and I have avoided speaking about it, because I shrank from giving you pain. But I feel it is best, once for all, to tell you frankly where I stand, so that there need be no misunderstanding between us.

You know that ever since I began to travel extensively, and visit foreign lands all around the world, I have employed nearly all my spare time in Biblical and theological studies, being led to this by observation of the varied interpretation of Scripture. In time, I adopted the Plymouth Brethren's system of *literal* interpretation, believing that, if God gave a revelation to man, it must be one that each man could understand for himself, without the intervention of any ecclesiastical or other human authority. I believed, therefore, that "God's word" meant what it said, and was not to be ingeniously twisted, its surface meanings ignored, and promises to the Jews "spiritualized" into prophecies of the Christian Church. I found that Christ promised his disciples that the Spirit should lead them "into all truth"; and it followed, from Protestant interpretation, that the prayerful student of the Bible, in whom, according to our theory, the Holy Spirit dwells, must learn the Bible's true teaching. Intercourse with numerous Christians, many of whom I was convinced prayed earnestly for the guidance of the Spirit, showed me that the Holy Spirit led each man to different and often opposing views: though one devout and highly educated Christian assured me that no one ever studied the Bible prayerfully without believing as he did, but I found that his present adherents numbered only two. The theory that these different views were like the varied aspects of a mountain from numerous points did not satisfy me, for a mountain never looks like a valley; and I began to doubt if it was possible that an omniscient God would give a *revelation* to man that would set all the world "by the ears" in their efforts to interpret it. The only solution to my mind was that each man's belief is determined by his own organization and surroundings. All religions are of human origin, Christianity not excepted.

Acquaintance with many lands, and conversation with "many men of many minds," showed me that, in all civilized or semi-civilized countries, there is a prevalent recognition of the great truths of morality, while ideas of religion vary. I saw less wickedness on the heathen shores of China, India, Java, and Sumatra than on the Christian wharves of New York and Boston or around the docks of London and Liverpool. Morality, therefore, is independent of religion, being the result of universal experience of the best methods of living.

But my early training and surrounding influences led me to suppress these convictions; and, for several years, I fought against my reason, restricted myself entirely to evangelical reading, and resolved not to doubt. At intervals, scepticism would revive, but by trampling on my intellect, plunging into religious work, and trying to accept the dogma that, as the finite cannot comprehend the infinite, the unintelligibility of a doctrine was a proof of its divinity, in this way I managed to preserve my faith. A visit to England and Germany rather unsettled me, until I buried myself again in "the faith of my fathers," and refused to acknowledge my own independence and right to think for myself, because the fathers and many living great men held and hold this faith. Finally, three years of travel, talk, and reading entirely emancipated my mind from the sway of the current Christian theology.

I believe that all things are subject to law, from the raindrop to the loftiest conception of the human brain. There is no supernatural interference. All will be accounted for as knowledge increases, and the reason why everything exists or acts will be shown. Therefore, as there are no miracles, there need be no prayer.

The study of the Bible, and comparing it with the sacred writings of other nations, convinces me that the Bible is a human compilation of the traditions, poetry, history, and religious ideas of the Jews in earlier and darker ages than the present. It is " God's word" only in the sense that what is good in all written, spoken, or secret thought may be called God's word. Its atrocities, indecencies, and incomprehensible dogmas are of the earth. I reject the orthodox doctrine of inspiration entirely.

The doctrines of evolution, in their main outlines, are now received by nearly all learned men, whether Christians or sceptics. The Bible says the world was made in six days by magic, man was perfect but sinned, Christ died to save a few, and soon God will destroy the world and punish the vast majority of men forever in hell. Evolution says the world is the product of a gradual development of matter, progressing through millions of years; man has arisen from lower animals, and they from inferior orders of animal and vegetable life down to the simplest atom. Analogy teaches that man will continue to rise, and, through the operation of the same laws, attain to a far higher, if not perfect development; for there must always be progress upward. So I have changed from a pessimist to an optimist; and, instead of ignoring this sin-cursed world doomed to destruction, I accept it as "the best world going," and one capable of improvement, it being my great aim so to advance my own nature and that of others that the world may be better for my life. Not the salvation of men's souls from hell, but the elevation of their hearts and minds, and the bettering of their social condition, is now my desire.

As to immortality, nothing is revealed to me, though many analogies encourage hope in a future existence. If there is no other life, we shall never know our loss in our dreamless sleep; and, if there is a future state, if we have lived well for this life, we shall be best fitted for another. One world at a time is enough; and, when another comes, it will then be time to take an interest in it.

I see no proof of a personal God, who sits up aloft and makes butterflies, counts hairs, and conjures up squalls to upset the boats of Sabbath-breakers; but I see an ever-active, unerring force in nature, working in the main for good, though painfully and mysteriously to "the creatures of a day."

The result to myself is that I am rid of the awful depression and gloom of the doctrine of hell, the nagging of conscience to pry into men's minds and know if they are "saved," the perplexing defence of the Hebrew Deity who ordered slaughter and rapine, the contempt of this life, and the Pharisaic conceit of the "elect." I now want to live, to enjoy what nature, art, and civilization supply, but all to the end of advancing humanity to a higher plane of virtue, knowledge, and happiness. I have lost nothing in motives to be good and do good, but have gained in freedom, hope, and gladness.

GAIN OR LOSS?

THE *Congregationalist* of November 30, 1881, under the above title, replied to "A Radical Avowal," published in the *Index* of November 10. It appeared to me easy to give satisfactory answers to the criticisms; but, having no desire for controversy, especially with so respected an old friend, I decided not to reply.

Numerous letters, some of them anonymous and not a few abusive, show that the readers of the *Congregationalist* consider that my positions have been utterly overthrown; and some of these dear, good people allow me only the alternative of demonism or an unbalanced mind as explanations for my opinions. Therefore, I feel it a duty, to myself at least, to see if I can "give a reason for the (unbelief) that is in me."

After stating my position as fairly as a brief abstract of my words would permit, the *Congregationalist* says it is "characterized, in nearly equal degree, by inconsistency, unfair statement, and hasty inference." The first inconsistency is the denial of a personal God, and yet saying "all things are subject to law"; for the editor says, "if there be law, the very conception necessarily implies a lawgiver." My words were, "I see no proof of a personal God, who sits up aloft and makes butterflies, counts hairs, and conjures up squalls to upset the boats of Sabbath-breakers." This is the kind of God I was "brought up on," a being who consciously superintends the formation of every insect, who notes and influences all the details of each human life, and who takes vengeance on sinners through "special providences." Many still believe in such a God, and draw the belief from the Bible. As opposed to this idea of a supreme being, I say, "I see an ever-active, unerring force in nature," and "all things are subject to law." "There is no supernatural interference." Many intelligent religious teachers call the force, which works in an orderly method throughout nature, God. They personify the principle of action which pervades existence; but this personal God is a great first cause, who endowed matter with the presence of force and the principle of development, by which all events spring from preceding causes, and who only acts through the successions of cause and effect, never exercising his will in an arbitrary way. My only purpose was to deny the existence of such a being as the Hebrew Jehovah or Calvin's God, who walked and talked with men, who destroyed them purposely with flood and fire and earthquake and plague, who turned a woman into salt, made an ass speak, killed fifty thousand and seventy men for looking into the ark, stopped the sun and moon in the heavens that a "Hebrew filibuster" might slaughter the Canaanites, saved a drowning prophet in a whale's belly, and who makes eternal decrees for the salvation of some, and allows others to inhabit an eternal hell.

What "God" is I am not wise enough to say. I am only sure he is not what the Hebrew writers imagined him to be. But, even had I denied the existence of any principle which can be called God, it is not inconsistent to speak of law. Webster gives nine definitions of *law*. The third is: "(Nature.) The regular method or sequence by which certain phenomena or effects follow certain conditions or causes, as the *law* of gravitation, a geological law, the laws of physical descent, of trade, etc.; the uniform methods or relations according to which material and mental forces act in producing effects, or are manifested in phenomena; a norm or rule for the working of a force: hence, any force, tendency, profession, or instinct, whether natural or acquired; as, the law of self-preservation, etc."

If *law* may be defined as "a rule for the working of a force," or the regular method of cause and effect, a materialist, who believes in no existence save that of eternal matter, may as consistently speak of the laws of the universe as may a Christian theist. This play upon words is a stock argument with theologians, but an honest consideration of the customary use of language shows it is a mere verbal quibble.

I claim, therefore, that, though I deny a personal God, who now consciously acts, creates, and repeats Bible wonders, I may consistently personify the force of evolution as God, and have an infinitely superior being to worship than the one described by Jewish and Christian poets, historians, and philosophers. Or, if I profess to believe in the eternity of matter, and that it is self-acting, I may consistently speak of the regular method of its working as *law*.

My second inconsistency is rejecting "the theorem that the Bible is a revelation to man, on the ground that it is inconceivable that any such thing can be true as to whose interpretation there is radical difference," forgetting that men differ about "philosophy, politics, medicine, and the like"; and it is asked, "Will he therefore affirm there is nothing which men can trust?"

I reply, There is nothing that men can trust, as an infallible revelation from God, about either religion, "philosophy, politics, medicine, and the like." When God reveals philosophy, idealists and materialists will agree; when he reveals politics, monarchists and republicans, free-traders and protectionists, will cease to quarrel; when he reveals medicine, allopathists, homœopathists, rubbing and electric doctors will adopt an harmonious system of treatment; and, when he reveals religion, the one hundred and sixty sects of Protestants, the Roman and Greek Churches, Mohammedans and Buddhists, will cease to revile each other, and will unite upon one theology. The illustration the *Congregationalist* gives to prove my inconsistency is all the evidence I ask to demonstrate the human origin of religion. Men admit that all knowledge of "philosophy, politics, medicine, and the like," has been slowly gained by the experience of man and his own toilsome efforts, unaided by any supernatural power; but they say religion has been revealed to man direct from a perfect omniscient God. We find, however, that men are no more agreed about religion which has been revealed than about science which has not been revealed. Of what advantage, then, is revelation? And is it not derogatory to God to suppose he could *reveal* what men cannot understand? The fact that men differ about religion, philosophy, politics, and medicine, proves that God has never given direct positive instruction upon these subjects. I cannot retort that the *Congregationalist* is "inconsistent," for such reasoning is consistent with the style of many of its arguments; but I may say it is illogical, when it maintains that the fact that men differ about unrevealed science is a reason why they may differ about revealed religion, for I assert that a *revelation* from an infinite God would compel the united assent of human minds. It seems, to my mind, to prove that religion rests on just the same authority as science,—namely, human experience and research; and God has never spoken about religion in any way that he may not be said to have talked politics or given medical lectures. "The Lord spake unto" Solon and Galen as truly as unto Moses. When men recognize the truth that religious ideas have no higher authority than medical ideas possess, they will become as charitable about theological differences as they now are about varying medical theories. Will it not be a social improvement?

The next charge is, "He seems to us unfair in statement, whenever he undertakes to describe what is Orthodox." My words are quoted, "The Bible says the world was made in six days by magic; man was perfect, but sinned; Christ died to save a few; and soon God will destroy the world, and punish the vast majority of men forever in hell." The editor then remarks, "We have studied the Bible for years with earnest care, but we have never found either of these statements in it; and, with a considerable acquaintance with Orthodox men, we know of none who would be willing to accept either as true."

This denial that the Bible teaches what I affirm it does, to use a sea phrase, struck me flat aback.

Can it be that for thirty years I studied the Bible, and understood it to teach things which nobody else finds there? If so, only one verdict can be given against my intelligence. But, if even a few men of good judgment and fair education have interpreted the Bible as I have, then it is the marvel of marvels that God should write a book expressly to give information on certain subjects, and, when some intelligent men decided what it taught, others equally intelligent should say it teaches no such thing. A governor of Massachusetts who should issue so obscure a proclamation would be elected to stay at home.

Fortunately for my self-assurance, I know many men whom the *Congregationalist* would pronounce orthodox and intelligent, who have found all these statements in the Bible. But let the book speak for itself. In Genesis, first chapter, we read that God created the present form of the world, its land, seas, vegetable and animal life, sun, moon, and stars, and man, in six days of evenings and mornings. In Exodus xx., 11, we read, "For in six days the Lord made heaven and earth, the sea and all that in them is."

Within a late period, learned men have discovered that the world was not made all at once in this complete condition, but through vast ages it has gradually been assuming its present forms and life. Theologians, therefore, tell us these days, each of which Scripture says was an evening and a morning, were really long periods. If the Bible is God's word, I prefer to take God's statement, as my Orthodox and not unlearned father did, who once said to me substantially: "This day-period theory is not consistent with a common-sense treatment of the Bible language. I prefer to hold to the plain words of God that he made the world in six days; and, though I cannot reconcile it with what are called geological facts, I believe some day science will come back to Moses." I have at hand literature showing that scholarly men hold in the same way to the literal day theory, and it will not be denied that the Church in all ages before the nineteenth century has followed this teaching. If God's people of to-day do not find it, they must admit that God allowed his church for many centuries to be deceived by false words of his,—a libel upon perfection.

God made the world by magic; that is, by "occult and superhuman agency." He made it "out of nothing" and said, "Let there be," and "there was."

We have found my first statement in the Bible as an average man would understand it. Now for the second, "Man was perfect, but sinned." In Genesis i., 27, it says, "So God created man in his own image, in the image of God created he him." I used to believe that this meant that man was perfect; but, since I have seen the imperfection of the Old Testament representations of Jehovah, I cannot so regard it, though I think it was the intention of the writer to give the impression that man was made perfect. If the *Congregationalist* will admit that the Hebrew God was imperfect, I must confess that his image will be faulty. As man's sin is spoken of on nearly every page of the Bible, I need not say this can be found there.

"Christ died to save a few." Now, I am in danger from theology. Men have battled for centuries as to whether Christ's atonement was limited or infinite; and the factions have made a kind of compromise, saying it is infinite in design, but limited in extent. Christ died for all, but only a part are saved. It is the practical effect of Christ's death that I refer to; and he said, "Narrow is the way which leadeth unto life, and few there be that find it." "He that believeth not shall be damned," and very few believe. Principal Dawson says of nominal Christians that God would call only two per cent. Christians. When one asked Christ, "Are there few that be saved?" he replied, "Many will seek to enter in, and shall not be able." He said, "Except a man be born again, he cannot see the kingdom of God." Certainly, but few are born again in the Orthodox sense. How then can Orthodoxy deny that but few will be saved? The good taste and intelligence of this age are limiting hell and expanding heaven; but the fact remains that the Church until recent years has found in the Bible the teaching that "God will punish the vast majority of men forever in hell."

"God will soon destroy the world." The *Congregationalist* and the post-millenarians say this cannot happen for a thousand years; but the pre-millenarians, among whom are such able Orthodox ministers as A. J. Gordon, H. M. Parsons, and Brooks of St. Louis, not to mention D. L. Moody and the numerous evangelists of this school, believe the first stage of this destruction may be ushered in at any moment by the appearance of Christ, "taking vengeance on them that know not God." Multitudes of Christians are looking for the coming of the Lord and "the end of the world" in its present condition. They see that the disciples were taught by Christ to expect this in their own day, and that all the teaching of the New Testament shows that this "hope" inspired its writers.

Perhaps the *Congregationalist* meant this denial for a joke. I can hardly believe it to be serious, though a joke would be so incongruous with its usual staid demeanor in theological discussions. But the second part of its assertion I am prepared to admit,—"With a considerable acquaintance with Orthodox men, we know of none who would be willing to accept either [of these statements] as true." Men are becoming too intelligent to accept these doctrines as true; but there they stand in the Bible, and millions of readers in the past have believed them, and many do still. After hearing a number of ministers in the neighborhood of Boston, I once wrote to the *Congregationalist*, asking "Is Christ preached?" I stated that I heard no allusion to man's sinfulness and need of a Saviour. The old-fashioned gospel of sin, hell, and atonement, as I had been instructed to read it in the Bible, which I still find there and which my father and brother faithfully preached, I have found to be tacitly ignored in the Congregational pulpits of cultured societies. Ministers have ceased to believe it, or even to find it in the Bible, by the exercise of ingenious methods of criticism especially designed to bring God's truth "up to the times." They are right to ignore these false notions; but, when they consistently explain their reasons for doing so, they are usually dismissed from their pulpits. I know whereof I speak when I say there are Congregational ministers of high standing who are thorough disciples of the evolution philosophy, who have lost every atom of belief in the inspiration of the Scriptures according to the definitions of creeds, who read the Old Testament with only the same credence that they give to Herodotus and Josephus and Eusebius, and yet by a discreet reticence, a use of old phraseology in a private sense with mental reservations, they maintain their status, and their hearers have no conception of their true belief. They are good and sincere men; they never utter what to their minds in their private understanding is false; but they know that people are not yet generally prepared to receive the truths which modern science has revealed, and they believe that the highest usefulness is subserved by this suppression of their convictions. Others see the light, and know that scholarly criticism has disproved the authenticity and genuineness of many of the books of the Bible, but early training and present surroundings make them shut their eyes and murmur the maxims of their youth: "The finite cannot comprehend the Infinite." "Reason must yield to faith." "God's thoughts are higher than ours." "If we could understand all God's words, it would throw doubt on their divine origin." And they trample on their intellects, as multitudes like myself have done and are still doing, to preserve their faith. My "evidence" of this is asked for. My reason told me years ago that Christianity was merely the best form of morality and religion that the human mind had been able to develop, and its literature was only the best religious writings of men. The difference between them and all other religions and sacred books was only one of degree, not of kind.

I yielded to early training so far as resolutely to *trample on my intellect*,—there is no other word for it,—and for years I buried myself in the Bible and Orthodox commentaries, upon the theory that the Christian must be "a man of one book." And so he must. A truer word was never uttered. If he could read this book as he reads his newspaper, with intelligence and common sense, he would see it in its true light as a human compilation of Jewish literature; but the bias of education, church, and commentator is too strong, and it becomes God's word, which only theologians can harmonize. Men therefore become the mental slaves of teachers who have had a life-training in the art of defending preconceived theories formulated by their ancestors. It would be a wonder if such ingenious effort did not produce some seemingly plausible arguments. These teachers are sincere. I was sincere, in spite of my substratum of doubt. Men are unconsciously biassed by their interests. The manufacturer is a protectionist, but the farmer and sailor are free-traders; and the minister is a Calvinist or Unitarian, or anything between, as his environment may determine.

More honest avowal of doubt is a duty which ministers will soon awaken to. They now hinder advancement by fearing to allude to the researches of the ablest scholars of the day, which they privately delight in, but feel it inexpedient to make public.

But I must not neglect the charge of "hasty inferences." Morality, I claim, exists independently of religion, being the result of universal experience. Then why, asks the *Congregationalist*, is the stay-at-home farm laborer more moral than the travelled sailor? If the world lasted but one generation, this question might apply to the case. But the dissolute sailor dies an early and loathsome death in a hospital, and the farm laborer lives to a green old age in tolerable health and comfort. This experience teaches the next generation that drunkenness and licentiousness are injurious, and, in time, further experience so impresses this fact upon society that commands are issued against these practices " in the name of God." These theories are too well defended by learned philosophers to be called "hasty inferences" of mine.

The other " hasty inference" is my assumption that " the Holy Spirit leads men to different and often opposing views." " How does he know it is the Holy Spirit?" it is asked. In this way:—Jesus said to his followers : " When he, the Spirit of Truth, is come, he will guide you into all truth. . . . How much more shall your heavenly Father give the Holy Spirit to them that ask him? . . . He shall teach you all things." In the Epistles, the indwelling of the Holy Spirit in believers is too frequently asserted to need quotation. The divine injunctions for the gaining of religious knowledge are " Search the Scriptures," and " If any man lack wisdom, let him ask of God." Prayerful study of Scripture is therefore generally accepted by Protestant Christians as God's channel of enlightenment to man. I was brought up among sincere, godly men, who read the Bible on their knees, and taught me that God's truth embraces everlasting punishment of all unbelievers in Christ, the election of a few to be saved, the baptism of infants, the keeping of the Sabbath, a select ordained ministry of preachers, a post-millennial advent of Christ, the spiritual or symbolical interpretation of prophecy, and other dogmas. During voyages to the East Indies, I became intimate with English missionaries holding some forms of the doctrines of the Plymouth Brethren. They were godly, self-sacrificing men, intelligent, and wonderfully familiar with the Scriptures. They studied "the Word" with special prayer for the Holy Spirit; and, if the Bible promises are true, they must have possessed it. Here was the result: The Bible taught them adult baptism, the abrogation of the "Sabbath," liberty of ministry for all believers according to their gifts (not their licenses), the pre-millennial advent and near coming of Christ, the literal interpretation of prophetic writings, and so on. My own prayerful study made me see that the Bible, read as it seemed to me God's word to man should be read, gives much support to these views; for God would not give a "revelation" in unintelligible allegories. If he speaks, he means what he says. Afterward, I came across men praying for the Spirit, who found the doctrine of annihilation of the unbelieving; and I met others who saw a limit to eternal punishment, and some who denied the deity and the atonement of Christ. Hell was my strong point, as became the son of the champion of the "Scriptural Argument for, and the Reasonableness of Future Everlasting Punishment." But here were believers in the inspiration of the Bible praying for the Holy Spirit's guidance, and disproving eternal hell from the very words of the Bible. In dismay, I cried, Of what use is such a word of God and such a Holy Spirit? Man's word, inspired only by man's spirit, teaches me when it pretends to, and men agree upon its meaning. If God's word is true and my observation of men is worth anything at all, some of these men who hold opposing views are led by the Spirit, therefore the Spirit teaches error. This is impossible, therefore God's word is not infallible.

If this is a hasty inference or is illogical, if some one will kindly demonstrate it by some argument other than the Orthodox one,—"You are mad or possessed with the devil,"—I shall welcome it, for this is the root of scepticism with me. Let me repeat and condense my argument. The revelation of an infinite God must convey to men truths which they will understand alike. The Bible is said to be a revelation from God. Good, intelligent men understand it differently. Therefore, the Bible is not the "word of God."

One point more. It is denied that "Christianity ignores the sinful world as incapable of improvement." Bible Christianity does,—not that which now prevails most generally,—though the growing pre-millennial creed is decidedly pessimistic. The Bible calls Christians out of "the world," warns them not to "love the world," reminds them that all will "be burned up," tells them not to "lay up treasure," but to "wait for their Lord." My own sense of consistency has in the past weakened my interest in either the material advancement or the pleasures of the world. Spiritual growth and salvation from hell were the only worthy objects of concern in this rapidly ending age. How could I dance and smoke and go to theatres, as many Christians do, while the multitude of men around me were passing into ceaseless doom! I helped to start a young men's society in the church, "for the moral, social, and literary improvement of the members and their enlistment in Christian work." The pastor was president. We started a night school and a prayer-meeting, which were soon abandoned; and the meetings became jovial entertainments, with violin and piano, songs, readings of Shakespeare and

Handy Andy, and finally the erection of a theatre stage in the lecture-room of the church, and the performance of "Bardell *vs.* Pickwick" in costume. Believing the Bible to be the word of God, I could not approve of this, and left the society. Seeing the Bible to be the word of man, I now say, Do what will make you better and happier now, in church and out of it; take care of your body and mind, and your "soul" will take care of itself. I do not deny that Christians enjoy life and believe in "the world," but I say they do so in spite of their creeds.

I must congratulate the *Congregationalist* and its friends that they have ceased to believe the teachings of the Bible as they were understood by the last generation of Christians. The sermons which I read or hear from Orthodox pulpits show that the most scholarly ministers are adopting the religion of evolution, which scientists and liberal thinkers have propounded, and quietly ignoring miracle and dogma, they add to this a sentimental and exaggerated estimate of the character of Jesus. This they call Christianity, and preach as though it had never been anything else. Heresy hunters are turned off by this enthusiastic loyalty to the person of Jesus. Greatly was I astonished to hear Boston's most talented Congregational minister declare that the Eden stories were allegories, and in their literal sense were offensive to reason and conscience. Would that more ministers would show such "courage of conviction"! Such *consistency* would relieve them from *unfair statement* and save the hearers from the *hasty inference* that the preachers are still "Orthodox."

I have been treated with more courtesy by the *Congregationalist* than heretics often receive; and I appreciate the kindly-intentioned desires for my restoration to the faith, though their fulfilment I should only regard as a calamity. I have lost a superstitious belief which I know has been injurious to me. All else is gain, unless my position loses for me the regard of the good *Congregationalist*.

HUMAN RELIGION.

Wherever we travel, we find that religious beliefs are as varying as the conditions of men, and that there is a correspondence in quality between the faith of the heart and the intelligence of the mind. Men's religious beliefs are elevated and rational in proportion to their enlightenment upon general topics. This fact has sometimes been interpreted as a proof that a man's religion determines his complete state, and that nations are high or low in the scale of civilization in accordance with the elevation of their creeds. Observation, however, convinces one that religion is not the cause, but the effect, of the education of the mental faculties. The Bushman of South Africa comprehends all of God that his untutored mind is capable of receiving, while the educated modern philosopher soars into the transcendental theories that are incomprehensible to the ordinary intellects of civilized lands. The proof of this lies in the fact that the improvement of the intellect always precedes an advance in the religious creed among races of men, though the stimulus given to the mind by the statement of a nobler faith quickens the faculties, and sometimes makes both advances appear coincident. Polytheism, or idolatry, is abandoned for monotheism, or the worship of one God, when the savage learns enough of science to know that the sun is not a fiery dragon, and that all the forces of nature are not so many demons. If the higher religion is given him by authority before the facts of nature, upon which it is based, are made known, he soon degrades it to the level of his former creed. Thus, Roman Catholicism gains many followers in heathen lands simply by a change of idols and the superior sensuousness of its rites. The Chinaman worships the statue of the Virgin Mary instead of that of Joss or Buddha, and experiences no mental alteration, whereas the effort of Protestant Christianity to overthrow idolatry is based upon reason, and its progress is therefore toilsome and slow. That religious belief depends upon the intellect is evidenced by the different interpretations given to the same faith by its followers. The ignorant Persian worships fire as his god, and firmly believes it to be the supreme power. But an intelligent Parsee in Bombay once said to me, " Me no worship fire, me worship mighty God, but me worship him through fire." The ignorant Romanist is on a level with the idolater in his reverence for the objects adored in his faith, but the educated man knows they are only symbols of spiritual truths : each makes his religion to suit his capacity. The chicken-stealing member of the African Church of the Southern States has a conception of Christianity as widely different from that of the graduate from a theological seminary as is the range in the capacity of their brains and the difference in their culture. One of these devout negroes thus related his conversion to my brother, who was for a time his pastor. I will not attempt to imitate the negro dialect.

"I had been thinking a good deal about religion, and at last I had a dream one night. I thought I was on board of a ship, and a big monkey came and chased me all around the deck. I got into the rigging and climbed up the mast just as fast as I could go, but the monkey came after me; and when I got away up to the top of the mast, he was just going to put his paw on me, when I fell off and tumbled away down to the deck. Then, I woke up, and found out that I'd got religion." His escape from the monkey gave him "joy and peace in believing."

A sailor, who was converted under my influence at sea, told me that, while in great distress on account of his sins, he turned into his bunk, and, falling asleep, dreamed that he had a pet animal in his arms. He was pursued by the devil; and, just as he was going to fall into his clutches, he tossed the animal to him, and made his escape. He awoke feeling happy, and at once told all the ship's company he had become a Christian. Another sailor, of more education, dreamed the end of the world had come and he was wading knee-deep in a fiery river : this so impressed him that he soon after "gave his heart to God," in order to secure his eternal safety. I recall the conversion of another person of superior attainments, who for some years had been repelled from embracing religion by the representation of God as a consuming fire. When led to realize that God loved her, she said, "Then, I will love him." She became a Christian. When asked for a statement of her belief, she wrote out the following: "God loves me, and therefore I love him. Loving us, he wishes our greatest and eternal happiness ; therefore bids us keep his commandments. Because we love him, we try to keep his commandments and bring forth the fruits of the spirit, so that, becoming like him, we may be fitted to enjoy his company, which is heaven." She knew nothing of conviction of sin or atonement. Others "experience religion" by feeling guilty, dreading the wrath of God, and accepting Jesus as the Saviour, through faith in his blood shed for them. Thus, Christianity is a different religion to different believers in it. Each adapts it to his own bent of mind.

The Bible statement, "God made man in his own image," is therefore rightly reversed, and we say, "Man makes God in his own image," and it is true that "an honest God is the noblest work of man"; for, as a man thinketh in his heart, so is he, and the conception each forms of the Deity shows the highest capacity and aspiration of his own nature. Many will admit that religions owe their origin to the fears and hopes of men, if we except their own religion. All are of human invention except their own, which came direct from heaven. God spoke to Confucius, Zoroaster, Gautama, Moses, Paul, Mohammed, Swedenborg, and Joe Smith,—so the follower of each claims, but denies that he spoke to any of the others. Among the followers of Moses and Paul, called "Christians," a difference exists about the interpretation of these words of God, each claiming to be the custodian of the truth. The Roman Church, the Greek Church, the one hundred and sixty sects of Christians in the United States and one hundred and forty-six in England, each believes itself to have the mind of the Spirit, that Christ promised should lead his followers into all truth. A leading light among the "Brethren" in England seriously told me that he never knew any one to study the Bible prayerfully without accepting his views as to the order and standing of the Church : others studied, but not prayerfully. Yet this good man had quarrelled with the other leaders of his sect, and set up a separate meeting of his own. Each believed he had the infallible guidance of the Holy Ghost and possessed a knowledge of *the truth*. But their bitter expressions of disapproval of each other's divinely received views almost brought their quarrels into the civil courts. When asked, "Why, if the Brethren have the real truth of God, do they not give the divine evidence of unity?" his answer was: "When Saul and Barnabas were set apart for the work of the ministry by the Holy Ghost, Satan at once proceeded to sow dissension between them. He doesn't trouble himself to annoy professors of false creeds; but as he saw Saul and Barnabas about to engage in spreading the true faith, and therefore attacked them, so he now sees the true Church of God in the Brethren, and uses every effort to disperse them. The fact that there is more dissension among the Brethren than among almost any of the sects of Christendom is only a proof that they hold the truth whose destruction Satan deems most vital to his cause." This came from no common man, but from one noted for his learning, skill, piety, and self-sacrifice. But no utterance has done more to convince me that his religion is from man, not from God. God is not the author of confusion. Men sincerely pray for the Spirit to lead them into the right view of the written word of God, and each gets a different result. Each is equally sure of his own sincerity and conscientious search, and denounces the views of all others as error. Who shall decide what is right? No one is fitted to be judge in his own cause. No Christian can be accepted as an infallible arbiter, when he tells us all religions are human conceptions except Christianity; and no member of a Christian sect is good enough authority for the assertion that his sect only reads the Bible aright. He is assuming the infallibility which he denounces the Pope and the Romish Church for claiming. The only fair tribunal to which can be referred the claim of Christianity to be the one divinely revealed religion, is the great and increasing body of men, who, in all civilized lands, are devoting their lives to the study of the facts of nature and society and the critical research of the records of each in past ages. Christianity, as God's sole truth, must stand or fall by its accord with the facts which are scientifically established.

The records of nature have now been found to reveal an orderly and progressive system of the development of matter and mind into its present forms, extending through vast ages, proving the Mosaic story of creation to be untrue, and placing it among the myths of earlier days of the human race, which are found to abound in the traditions or literature of all people. This orderly progress of nature reveals an unvarying method, which makes every effect the result of preceding natural causes; and the violations of its methods, called "miracles," are unsupported by sufficient evidence to warrant their belief. Every miracle of which circumstances have permitted a scientific examination has been disproved, and shown either to be a fraud or to be the result of a law of nature known or fairly supposed. The miracles of our days are now on the eve of solution by the discovery of the laws of psychology and animal magnetism, which many learned men believe will in time solve all that is not fraudulent in the phenomena of Spiritualism. Historical study shows the Bible wonders to be of the same character as those recorded in the religious books of all other nations; and literary criticism proves it to abound in errors, inconsistencies, and contradictions, showing it to be the word of man. The Christian scheme of theology must therefore take its place in the order of the development of human thought, and in time give place to the next system which the advancing mind of man evolves; that, in turn, to be improved upon as knowledge of nature and the control of her forces increases.

A study of the theories of evolution leads most people to accept them, and the only certain way in which one can maintain his belief in the religious faith he has adopted by the accident of birth is never to question it. One who attempts to submit his creed to rational tests, as he treats everything else in life, must either become an entire sceptic of the supernatural, or else fall into the arms of an authoritative Church and accept all its dogmas without question. The churchman who reasons for himself is lost to his religion. This is well illustrated by the careers of the Newman brothers, who, in the search for truth, have become, one a cardinal in the Romish Church, the other an ultra-rationalist.

While firmly believing that all religious ideas proceed from men's minds, and not from direct external revelations from God, we may recognize the law of evolution in the development of religious thought as the same which produces all variation and progress in nature. Religion as well as science is the result of the working of the infinite power which inspires matter. These, and all things, in this sense, are "of God." *All* religions are therefore "of God." "God" has developed erroneous ideas in science and false notions in religion; but they were steps in progress, and the infinite force is slowly evolving newer and truer conceptions from men's minds. Religion is as truly of human origin as astronomy and mechanics, and as truly divine as geology and meteorology. "God" has revealed religion as truly and in the same manner as he has revealed ship-building.

IS THE BIBLE THE WORD OF GOD?

CRITICISM of the Bible is considered to belong to an elementary stage of rationalism, and is scarcely tolerated by many advanced thinkers who have far outgrown discussion upon so trite a theme. But a book that has an annual circulation of three million copies is still deserving of attention; and it is possible there are some readers to whom one more statement of reasons which led an inquirer to the rejection of the inspiration of the Bible may be beneficial and interesting.

The Book of Genesis gives an account of the creation of the present condition of the world and all its forms of life in six days, man being formed complete and "grown up" out of the dust, and woman being made from the man's rib. Science proves this to be entirely untrue, and history shows the record to be on a par with various other legends of creation, which other races of men have made, though it is superior to most in one respect, the recognition of only one God. Theologians are desperately trying to save the Bible by ingenious theories, none of which, so far, will bear the scrutiny either of science or common sense. They make the days long periods, though this is in contradiction to the plain words of Scripture, and even then fails to solve the difficulty.

The second chapter of Genesis contains another legend of the creation, differing from the first in important particulars, but no more reconcilable with facts. It is now established in the opinion of scholars that the world is of immense age, and that man has existed upon the earth for a much longer period than the story in Genesis makes possible. The records of the earth itself contradict this legend. The nebular hypothesis, though still only a theory, accounts for the formation of the universe in accordance with all known facts ; and science discovers many uncontroverted evidences of the gradual progression of the earth and its inhabitants to their present form. Prof. Huxley asserts that the chalk cliffs of England, which are composed of the minute shells of sea animalcules, must have been at least ten thousand years in forming at the bottom of the ocean. They have slowly risen to the surface and subsided four different times, remaining exposed such long periods as to collect vegetable and animal life, whose remains tell their own story. A pious lady, to whom this was mentioned, excitedly exclaimed, " It was all made by God in one night." When asked if it was either reasonable or honest in God to create old bones, fossil plants, the rock debris from icebergs, and then cover them up in four successive layers to deceive man as to the earth's origin and to contradict his own story in Genesis, she was speechless. But the next day she said, "God says so, and I believe him."

There is a marvellous succession of forms in vegetable and animal life, and a connection between each grade so close as to suggest the probability and almost certainty that the higher forms have sprung from the lower. Anatomists tell us that the embryo of man appears successively to be identical with that of a plant, an animalcule, an oyster, a fish, a quadruped, a high form of mammal, an ape. If the individual passes through these forms, is it not probable that the race has likewise developed from these lower races? Anatomists also tell us that men have rudimentary tails, and it is observed that the disuse of an organ in animals tends to its disappearance. Why should God take the trouble to make a useless tail bone, when he formed Adam out of the dust? Is it not more likely that man has developed from a tailed animal? This theory is considered revolting by many, who think it less honorable to be an improved animal than a degraded God; but taste should not be an arbiter in the judgment of truth, though it is usually deemed nobler to ascend than to descend.

But leaving the question of creation, as one proceeds through the Bible, he is confronted on nearly every page with statements which offend either his reason or conscience. If any one wishes to see a statement of Biblical errors, let him read Paine's "Age of Reason," and with it let him take Bishop Watson's "Reply to Paine," and read what is considered by the orthodox an unanswerable defence of the Bible. Or, for a smaller work, let him take the "Lecture on the Bible," by Rev. Charles Voysey, published by the Index Association, Boston. It would be sufficient to read the Bible alone, to discover the falsity of the claims its friends make for it, were it not that educational prejudices are so strong one cannot easily treat the book as he does other literature. But let one take up the Bible as he does any modern book, and judge of its contents according to the impression made upon his faculties, and it seems impossible not to reject its claim to be the infallibly inspired word of God, and perceive it to be a compilation of Hebrew tradition and poetry made by men in darker ages than the present.

All the phenomena of witchcraft are now believed by scientists to be the products of natural laws. If they are right, is not God proved guilty of ignorance when he gave the edict, "Thou shalt not suffer a witch to live," and was it not a wicked ignorance which through this command has caused such countless murders and persecutions? Dr. Sprenger, in his "Life of Mohammed," estimates that nine million people have been put to death as witches during the Christian era. Blackstone said that to deny witchcraft was to deny revelation. How can the inspiration of this law stand the light of the present day? The issue is avoided only by denying the facts of scientific research and reviving the old belief in "being possessed of the devil." Prof. Phelps, of Andover, has consistently avowed this solution.

The atrocities of the Hebrew armies, done in the name and by command of God, the absurd wonders of Balaam, Gideon, Joshua, Samson, Elijah, Hezekiah, and Jonah, and the incomprehensible rhapsodies of the prophets, out of which learned and imaginative men can invent any theory they choose, are to a reflecting mind strong means of breaking down an inherited belief in the inspiration of the Bible.

But, admitting the Old Testament to be a human compilation, some think the New Testament can stand alone as the word of God. One of the first things that excites distrust here is the discovery that all the prophecies claimed as referring to Christ are found to be uttered about people or events of the times in which the writer lived, and that the application of them to Christ is either fraudulent or the use of an excessive poetic license. The story of the temptation in the wilderness is as hard to accept as that of the temptation of Adam and Eve in Paradise; and, if one begins to admit that any Bible stories are mere symbols, there is no end to the extent to which its text can be symbolized away.

A comparison of the different accounts of the resurrection of Jesus reveals discrepancies that no honest harmonizing can blend into consistency with the idea that God has told us the story. Nor would any English-speaking judge accept a fact upon such testimony in a court of law. Let each write out the stories in parallel columns, and decide for himself. The different genealogies of Jesus in Matthew and Luke; the incidents of the miraculous conception and birth; the star in the east; the slaughter of children by Herod, mentioned only by Matthew and unnoticed in history; the differing accounts of Saul's conversion; the miracle stories; the fact that Jesus is not mentioned by contemporary historians; the uncertainty as to who wrote the Gospels and when they were written,—all these things, and multitudes that it would be tedious to mention, prove the New Testament to be the word of man, and of less enlightened man than exists to-day.

The study of prophecy occupies many minds. Writers upon these subjects glean many disjointed passages, which, ingeniously matched together, make a wonderful testimony; but, when these passages are read in the Bible in their proper connection, they tell a different story.

If God inspired the writers of the Bible, it would also be necessary to the fulfilment of his purpose that he should superintend the compilation of its books by councils, its translation by scholars, and its interpretation by commentators. But the facts do not show that this has been done, as new versions would not be needed, nor would doctrinal quarrels exist. Has God allowed men for eighteen hundred years to accept the plain words of his revelation which teach future endless punishment, and is he now going to accommodate his *truth* to the culture of this century, and let up a little in the severity of the doctrine? Has the Holy Spirit, who came to guide into all truth, led men to believe error for eighteen hundred years because it was best for their minds; and, now that their mental calibre demands something different is he going to reveal "a new phase of truth," and allow men to modify the severity of the doctrine of hell? Will theologians admit that God gave a written revelation of the future destiny of men, which could not be understood till eighteen centuries of development evolved their own brilliant intellects? We can conceive of God as revealing truth progressively, as a child is taught at school, but not as teaching what is untrue, in order to prepare the way for the truth, centuries after his dupes have died.

It is a common saying, "You can prove anything by the Bible." Coincidences and far-away resemblances in different portions of the text have been made to do duty by expositors, as showing "the mind of the Spirit" in making the disjointed Scriptures an harmonious whole. At a Bible reading, I heard Harry Moorhouse explain the meaning of Christ's riding into Jerusalem on an ass's colt, after this manner: "In Job xi., 12, we read, 'For vain man would be wise, though man be born like a wild ass's colt.' The wild ass's colt is therefore an emblem of man. In Exodus xiii., 13, we read, 'And every firstling of an ass thou shalt redeem with a lamb; and if thou wilt not redeem it, then thou shalt break his neck.' Here, again, the ass's colt is the emblem of sinful man, who must be redeemed by the Lamb of God, or else perish forever. So, in Christ's entry into Jerusalem on an ass's colt, we see a symbol of the Redeemer and the redeemed entering into glory." This is making comparison "go on all fours"; but many hear such things and exclaim: "Wonderful! how the parts of the Bible fit into each other! Only God could have inspired writings in different ages which would display such a unity of design."

An intelligent Swedenborgian tells me why Jesus was laid in a manger. It was not because there was no room for him in the inn, but because God deliberately chose the manger to illustrate a truth. The horse is used in Scripture as an emblem of the understanding. He gets his food from the manger. God therefore put Jesus in the manger, to teach the world that he was the truth upon which the understanding must feed. The Bible is only an allegory. The story of creation and the formation of Adam is merely a figurative account of the condition of the Church at a certain period. The Bible is of no value to the Swedenborgians as a literal narrative, while to the Plymouth Brethren every word has a literal import in relation to some fact. Calvinists use both methods. If their doctrine can be supported by a spiritual interpretation of the text, that is clearly the right one; but, if it brings stronger evidence as a literal statement, that is clearly its true meaning. Often, they combine both systems, and make the text work both ways, by using its primary meaning as literal, and its secondary signification as spiritual. Of course, we are at liberty to find spiritual significance and suggestion in every one of nature's facts or author's words; but it is another thing to declare the author's true spiritual thought in an ordinary statement of fact, then found a doctrine upon it, and call it by the author's name, as though he intentionally founded it. This acceptance of the Bible as supernatural and these different systems of interpreting it are the foundation of all sectarianism. The learners in every other department of knowledge dispute as to the truth of the statements made by the writers in those sciences, but they do not differ materially as to what the writers intended to teach. In medicine, one author asserts the truth of allopathy, and another maintains homœopathy: disputes are vigorously carried on as to which is right; but there is no controversy as to what each writer intended to teach. Here is where the Bible differs from all other books. God is said to have written it, and the world is divided as to what it meant to teach; but every human writer on earthly knowledge succeeds in giving his readers an understanding of what he means to assert. If we were told God had given a revelation on medicine, would we receive it as divine, if it divided up the world into two hundred medical schools, many of them utterly opposed? Would not the real meaning of God's message about medicine be understood substantially alike by all? Would any man be respected who could not tell his own mind upon medical subjects, so that his meaning could be perceived? When God writes on theology, Trinitarians, Unitarians, Swedenborgians, and all other sects, will find their occupation gone; and, when he writes on medicine, doctors will agree.

THE BIBLE A HUMAN BOOK.

WHY is it that differences of opinion upon earth-knowledge are regarded so much more leniently than differences upon theology? Bitter words certainly are waged between scientists, but social ostracism and denunciation of personal character seem to belong especially to religious controversy. The reason is that scientists know that all knowledge is the result of human research, but theologians claim a direct revelation from God to man about their doctrines. When they admit that knowledge of the unseen world has no other key than that which unlocks the secrets of visible matter; that all departments of learning are on an equal footing, each open to the full, free, and fearless investigation of man; that no supernatural information has ever been given by any supreme being upon any subject, but that all the attainments of man are the result of progressive steps,—then the earnest searcher for spiritual and religious truth will be no more despised than is the inventor, the chemist, or the electrician. They may still see God as the inspirer of matter, the wondrous power which enables man to take his toilsome, progressive steps into the realms of knowledge, even though they admit that he never revealed morality all at once from Sinai, nor his scheme of mercy in one dogma from Calvary, any more than he revealed the railroad in England or the telegraph in America. All have grown from man's gradual experience through the ages; and yet this is no less truly "of God," if by that name we mean the principal of action that pervades nature. God spoke as truly to Stephenson and Morse as he did to Moses and Paul. He said, Let railroad-trains run, and, Let words be telegraphed, just as truly as he said, "Thou shalt not steal." And he said it in the same way; namely, by working through matter in nature and in man's organism, until experience and observation made man perceive that theft was injurious to society, that steam could move carriages, and electricity could repeat motion.

If the Bible is recognized as a human book, it will become of more real value to man. Now, it is by many worshipped ignorantly, as a sort of fetich. Others injure their intellectual powers and lose their common sense in attempting to make the works of different writers in different ages tell one harmonious story, as though written by one being. Others, who find some repulsive and incredible things in the book, spurn the whole, because obliged to consider the book as a whole. If they were allowed to read the Old Testament as a record of the traditions, history, and poetry of a distant age, it would become an intelligible, interesting, and valuable book to them. If the New Testament could be admitted to contain the best portrayal of human excellence ever written by man, and the philosophies and theologies of the early centuries of this era, it would then be prized by such men for what it is worth; and no one will honestly deny its real value. Men find there eternal punishment for the many and salvation for the few. They are told it is God's Book, and they must accept every word; but they revolt against these words, and throw away the whole.

One of the most noted authors of our day told a friend that he grew up with very little knowledge of the dogmas of religion or acquaintance with the Scriptures. Marrying a Christian woman, he yielded to her entreaties to read the Bible. He perused it from Genesis to Revelation, then shut up the book, and said, "If you wish me to have any respect for your religion, never show me that book again." Its supernaturalism offended his reason and instincts; and, as he was told it was all God's truth and must be taken as a whole, he would have none of it. This man's books are read in every Christian family in the land, and his unbelief does not seem to disqualify him for pleasing and instructing others.

Another great difficulty in receiving the Bible as the word of God is the manner in which its books have been chosen. A large number of apocryphal books are known to have been excluded from the Old Testament, though quotations from some of them appear to be used by the apostles; and the New Testament is the result of the votes of councils, some Gospels and Epistles having been rejected, while other Epistles were retained by a bare majority, but all henceforth is the infallible word of God. When we revolt against inconsistency and error in it, we are told the finite must not judge the infinite, reason must give place to faith. But it is faith in the Christian Fathers that is needed.

Again, if God is God of the whole earth, and will have all men to be saved, even though he did not make Christ known until four thousand years after Adam sinned and brought doom to his race, why was not this word, which proclaims the fact, made intelligible to ordinary men, that they might not be the intellectual slaves of the learned hierarchy, who alone are professedly able to make a consistent story out of it? As it stands now, it is in no true sense a "revelation" to man; for scarcely two people can understand it alike. A God who had the intellectual powers of a modern college graduate could make a revelation that would not set all the world at variance in attempting to explain it; and he could find a way of making it known to the world, instead of confining its manifestation to an obscure and semi-barbarous people in a corner of the earth, leaving vast multitudes to perish ere the saving tidings could reach them. It is derogatory to infinite intelligence to call the Bible its "revelation."

Christ is said to have spoken in the Aramaic tongue, a language now extinct. His words were reported from mouth to mouth, were probably written in Hebrew, and after many years were translated into Greek. Their record was transcribed repeatedly; and the manuscripts, written several hundred years after the death of Christ, are now rendered into the English language. These words, passing through four languages, and subject to all the changes that gossips and copyists may have wrought, are now presented to us as the word of God, which determines our eternal welfare. Such a revelation is unworthy of an omnipotent being, who is conceived to have infinite perfection and who desires to convince men of truth; but it is a consistent act on the part of a God who hardened Pharaoh's heart, who is said to create evil, who said, "Make the heart of this people fat, and make their ears heavy, and shut their eyes; lest they see with their eyes, and hear with their ears, and understand with their heart, and convert, and be healed" (Isa. vi., 10), and of whom it is said, "God shall send them strong delusion, that they should believe a lie" (II. Thess.

ii., 11). It is conceivable that such a God should give a revelation that would be incomprehensible.

Literary research is constantly throwing light upon the human origin of the Bible and the pagan sources of its doctrines. The "Bible for Learners" revolutionizes the chronology of the Old Testament and its reputed authorships. Kuenen's "Religion of Israel" gives a masterly exposition of the details of these subjects, which is condensed in a work with the same title by Knappert. The oldest books are said to be Amos, Hosea, Zechariah (ix.–xi.), and the first twenty-seven chapters of Isaiah. The principal part of Deuteronomy was written about 620 B.C. Then, at about the time of the captivity in Babylon (586–538 B.C.), Jeremiah, Ezekiel, and the rest of Isaiah were written. After the return, Ezra brings to light (444 B.C.) "God's Law which was given by Moses." The Psalms and Proverbs are gradually collected together, histories and prophecies are compiled and written, nobody knows by whom. The apocryphal books follow, and the book of latest date in the Old Testament is thought to be Daniel. (See "The Growth of the Hebrew Religion," by W. C. Gannett, *Unity* office, Chicago.)

The author of "Supernatural Religion" claims to prove the spuriousness of the Gospels. The Oriental origin and human development of Christianity are shown in such works as Clodd's "Childhood of Religions," Johnson's "Oriental Religions," and Max Muller's "Origin and Growth of Religion." All the Christian dogmas are found in previous creeds in Egypt, Persia, and India, or in classic mythology. The miraculous-conception dogma was common among the ancients. Romulus was the son of Mars; Plato, of Apollo; Alexander, of Jupiter Ammon; Sosiosh, the Persian saviour, was born of a virgin, and will come to regenerate the world, preceded by two prophets. The Persians taught the doctrine of the resurrection, that the good will inherit the earth, and Ahriman and his angels will be purified in a lake of molten metal. One author says: "Every Christian dogma has its origin in a heathen rite. . . . . Christian theology is only a *potpourri* of pagan mythologies." Renan says, "Nearly everything in Christianity is mere baggage brought from the pagan mysteries." The coincidences in the lives and teachings of Jesus and Gautama Buddha have been remarked upon by many writers. Taylor says, "Everything of Christianity is of Egyptian origin." The fables of India and Persia were brought to Egypt, and recast. It is difficult to trace the exact origin of ideas, and learned men differ in opinion as to the birthplace of some dogmas, but this much is certain,—Bible theology was not an exclusive revelation to the Jews.

Many of our interpretations of Scripture and

much of their authority rest upon the assertions of the "Christian Fathers." If any one would gain a true estimate of the value of the testimony of these worthies, let him read of their lives and writings and superstitions, and he will be slow to accept their dicta about "God's Word." If one would see how legends originate and spread, and see a plausible suggestion for the existence of many of the Bible stories, he should read John Fiske's "Myths and Mythmakers," and S. Baring-Gould's "Curious Myths of the Middle Ages" and "Legends of Patriarchs and Prophets."

Modern research is throwing great light on the manner in which the present Bible was compiled. How a majority of one in a council of "Fathers" could make one book the infallible word of God, and a larger majority condemn another to be the word of man, is a mystery which it needs the authority of an infallible Church to make one believe. Pappus, in his "Synodikon," says all the Gospels were put under the communion table, and the inspired ones got up on the table, in answer to prayer. Stanley, in his "Eastern Church," alludes to this "tradition." But, whether this story is true or not, can it be that God's Word has been left by its author to drift about the world, subject to human alteration, to be finally rescued from a mass of literary rubbish by a council of men in a dark and superstitious age? This is not God's way, or at least not the way of a God whom this century can worship.

What a terrible waste of intellect there is in the world, arising from this assertion, that the Bible is the word of God and contains a harmonious system of final truth! When the powers that are now used to defend theories concerning the Scriptures are directed toward positive explorations of nature's secrets, how the world will spring forward! When theological seminaries become science schools, and look for truth in living facts, they will be greater boons to the world.

To my mind, the true theory of the Bible is that, on the principle of the survival of the fittest, the best and most helpful writings of men have been preserved; and the book is to be prized as an evidence of the working of the secret power of nature in men's minds, and also for whatever of truth it contains, according to present perceptions of the good. It is the bad use men have made, and are still making, of the Bible that has done harm. Interpreting men's sins and crude ideas as revelations of God's mind debases man. If men now find the Mosaic beginning and the Christian ending of the world, as portrayed in the Bible, to be opposed by science and sense, is it not more honoring to God and creditable to man to admit that there is no revelation save what men have slowly and painfully learned for themselves from nature's operations, while the race has been "toiling upward in the night" of ignorance and superstition? One revelation pervades all nature; and the students of this revelation have recorded their observations in Bibles, works upon natural history, and histories of man. The "Books of Moses," Hume's, Gibbon's, and Macaulay's histories, Humboldt's "Cosmos" and Darwin's "Origin of Species," contain men's perception of revealed facts. The Psalms of David, Bryant, and Longfellow, the Proverbs of Solomon, Æsop, Cervantes, and Franklin, the prophecies of Isaiah, Carlyle, and Emerson,—all contain "the word of the Lord"; and the latest is the truest and the best, because most in accord with known facts and present needs.

HUMAN IDEAS OF GOD.

THE idea of God has gradually developed in the human mind through stages corresponding to the intellectual condition of the race. . Graduating from the regions of fetichism and idolatry, the early Hebrew writers conceived of God as a powerful being who, by the might of his word, called everything into existence ready-made at a moment's notice, and controlled current events by direct supervision. At later periods, we observe changes in the names and nature of God. Ewald has noted distinctive names of the God of the five great periods of the history of Israel. He was Almighty to the patriarchs, Jehovah to the priests, God of Hosts to the kings, the Holy One to the prophets, and Our Lord to Judaism. We see an increasing approach of God to man from the Creator to the Leader, Rock, Fortress, Helper, until he is known as the Father. It may be said that God thus revealed himself progressively to the race, but it is harder to conceive of an omnipotent and omniscient God thus playing hide and seek with his creatures than it is to believe that men in each age have evidenced the nature and extent of their needs, desires, and aspirations by the conception they have formed of a supreme being. God is always the complement of the weakness of man. What man consciously lacks of perfection he attributes to God.

Down through the Middle Ages, we see a varying God, suiting the degree of light and darkness that pervaded the mental world. The Puritan made a stern God glorying in his decrees, in accordance with the resolute self-sacrificing devotion to the view of truth which inspired his own breast. And, now, Moody and his kindred evangelists are proclaiming the God of whom they have learned from the English "Brethren,"—a God of love, his attribute of vengeance softened to Justice, and all his characteristics put into a nineteenth-century dress. The Brethren evangelists have flocked over to America for fifteen years past, making the Young Men's Christian Associations their rallying points; and, telling their ardent disciples that they were "living by faith," their needs have been bountifully supplied by voluntary contributions "from the Lord." Through preaching services and Bible readings and the circulation of their literature, they have widely indoctrinated the associations and churches with the truths of a full and free atonement, assurance of salvation, the presence of the Holy Spirit, and the pre-millennial advent of Christ. They have been mostly good men, and have substituted a better and more Scriptural theology for that of the New England churches of the previous half-century. Moody's preaching only became noted and effective after he had been indoctrinated by Needham and Moorhouse. When you find an evangelist gaining converts by exposition of the Scriptures, not by sensationalism, you will usually discover the theology of the Plymouth Brethren as the inspiring influence. Their doctrines about prophecy prevail widely in the Church of England, and are spreading through the various sects of America. Their missionaries are all over the world, living by faith and preaching a "pure gospel," the needs of many being "supplied by the Lord," through George Muller, of Bristol.

My father came under these influences in his later years, and preached a sermon called "The Free Gift," which was considered such a contrast to the "hyper-Calvinism" which had previously characterized his preaching that it was printed and widely circulated by an enthusiastic parishioner who held the Brethren's theology. He afterward said to me on a voyage at sea, "If I could live my life over again, how differently I would preach!" He said he had proclaimed too much the terrors of the law, and alluded to certain good lady parishioners who had lived and died in gloom, feeling that they were lost sinners, as they felt no evidence that they belonged to the number of the elect. He said he had not made the gospel free enough. The sermons in his volume, "At Eventide," were written at this period, and breathe a milder spirit than those of his earlier ministry. His God changed as his mind mellowed.

If individual Christians are now questioned about God, it will be seen that quite different beings are worshipped under that name; each man creating his own mental image of the deity whom he loves, fears, or adores. We set up a standard and try to attain to it, and we call that standard God. One beauty of the Bible is that, being written by men of varied capacity in different ages, there are correspondingly varied views of God's nature, so that different temperaments will find something to suit their phases of mind. If God had written the book, it would have been consistent; and there would have been a pattern deity revealed, who, while more noble in design and elevating in influence, would not have been so comforting to imperfect creatures who enjoy a God "after their own hearts." The Delphic Oracle said, "The best religion is that of a man's own city."

Now comes science, and asserts that nothing has been made all at once, and that all the facts of creation are or will be accounted for by the theory of the evolution of matter. Everything now and in the past has grown or developed by slow stages from simpler forms, in accordance with laws which are just beginning to be clearly understood. There is no such thing as the "act of God," as that term has usually been understood; but every event, from the lightning's stroke to the mosquito's sting, is traceable to the workings of law. God never interferes by miracles or special providences, and it is only our ignorant and sluggish minds that seek such a solution for our baffled investigations into the subtle laws of nature. It is convenient to say "God did it," when we cannot explain a matter. Where knowledge ends God begins.

Some call this great law and force God, and rightly consider that it is a far loftier conception, to think of the Being who could originate matter and endow it with the properties of evolution, so that for ages it could work on without a single act of interference, and produce the wonderful diversity we now behold in nature, working in never-failing precision, than it is to enthrone one as the Supreme Being, who, like a necromancer, calls up what he wants upon emergencies; who takes a notion to have a new kind of butterfly, and makes it on the spot; who causes a profane man to step on a bit of orange peel and break his leg, and sends a tornado to an infidel village. These tell us we can know nothing of God beyond the revelation of his works, and must content ourselves with the investigation of secondary causes.

Others, having traced all the variations of matter back to a single atom, and believing that every form it has assumed can be accounted for by the workings of natural law, are averse to calling in the supernatural even here, and think that qualities inherent in matter may have initiated the first movements which have led to "differentiation." This leaves only the origin of matter to be accounted for, and some are daring enough to believe that the intellect of man will yet solve this problem. They claim that, as the most complex organism can be traced back to the simple cell, so the profoundest operations of the mind are the result of an unbroken ascent from the first instinctive effort of the lowest animalcule to propagate its species or obtain food, and this gradual development of mind can be followed through all the animal kingdom up to man, the difference between the mental operations of man and animals being differences of degree, not of quality. The ant, the horse, and the dog think the same kind of thoughts that men do, as far as their range of thought extends. The operations of mind are found to depend entirely upon physical organs, and can be suspended or altered by changes in the conditions of those organs. Anatomists and physiologists find a correspondence between the brain, the contour of the head, and the mental faculties, so that a man's or animal's mental powers and characteristics can be predicated from his physical formation. This chain of sequence is so well traced that it is made clear that the link between the brightest dog and the lowest Hottentot is closer than that between a Hottentot and a Newton. Wallace remarks that the faculties exercised by savages are very little above those of the animals. If mind, therefore, can be followed down to the first instinctive motions of the earliest forms of matter, and is proved to depend on the organism, may it not yet be shown that the first motion that signifies intelligence is as truly a development from the inherent nature of matter as is the growth of the structure? The assumption that there is an eternal distinction between mind and matter, and that it was necessary at some point for a God to step in and conjure the principle of mind into matter, would thus be shown to be false by the proof of the theory that matter has always possessed the principle of determining its actions which we call mind. May not mind be traced as truly in the vegetable world? When plants catch and devour insects, reach out tendrils toward supports, close their flowers in the shade or at the approach or touch of a person, may it not be called an operation of mind, as truly as when a dog answers the dinner bell or a man opens an umbrella when it rains?

Thus there is a mind or soul in all nature, and it is so connected with and inseparable from the outward form that they may be considered one, the mind, the later manifestation, being an inherent property of matter from its first existence.

These facts and theories either place God away back at the beginning of all things, and then leave the puzzle of his existence to be accounted for, or, ignoring any idea of a personal God, they consider the existence of matter as the only mystery to which we have not found a hopeful key. Nothing is arbitrary in the action of nature, implying an exceptional discrimination. As a general rule, the good and the bad reap the results of their acts in the long run. Just so many accidents of a given kind occur during certain periods under similar circumstances. The number of suicides in London in each decade and the number of mis-directed letters in certain periods is about the same. There is no event in the world of mind or matter which it is not easier to account for as the result of natural consequences than as being the direct act in each case of a superintending God. The blast of lightning from a clear sky, which struck twenty men resting under an oak-tree, was not specially directed by a God with reference to those men. But a sufficient knowledge of natural law could show a chain of causes extending back for ages, which required that flash to gleam and that it should strike that tree; and laborers are apt to rest under trees at noon in hot weather. As the mind revolts from the idea of a God who deliberately ordains some men to eternal life of his own free will and leaves others to perish, so it rejects the thought of a being who consciously distributes the accidents and ills of life, and orders the daily warfare and destruction which pervades all orders of nature.

If, then, it can be shown that all the present forms of existence may be accounted for by natural laws, reason obliges us to prefer this theory to that of the special creation of the various orders of life by the magical word of a Supreme Being. Man's ignorance has always taken refuge in the act of God as an explanation of what could not be understood. God was supposed to cause cholera, plague, and small-pox by direct exercise of his will, until the germ theory of disease showed that these calamities could be accounted for by natural laws. God made the lightning, in popular estimation, till Franklin flew his kite and brought it down from heaven to the realm of nature. God caused storms, rains, and droughts, till the science of meteorology showed the power of natural causes to produce these effects, and foretold their occurrence. So, in earlier ages, the mysteries of life were conveniently referred to God; but, now, we see the laws of nature satisfactorily explaining all the facts of existing forms, and we only refer back to God the origin of matter and force. This is merely saying that as yet we are ignorant of the first cause of all existence; but, having resolved so many of the acts of God into intelligible processes of nature, does not analogy suggest that what is still unknown may yet be discovered by the advancing mind and unceasing investigation of man? Thus there is no "unknowable," and no limits need be placed upon man's mental progress, nor need any barriers be raised to stop his researches.

It is imprudent to express a decided opinion upon these theories about God, upon which the wisest of men are at variance. None of them solve the great mystery of existence. We are all groping through the dim day-dawn toward God, if, haply, we may find him. My only object in writing is to show that the ideas of God in the Bible are human conceptions, just as are the ideas of theologians and philosophers of to-day. They are not authoritative; but they are instructive, and show an orderly progression which ranks them among the evidences which pervade all orders of nature of a development through which an inscrutable force, or "God," is working.

Many, from policy or conviction, are making a compromise with Christianity as to belief in God, and thus avoid an open rupture. They say, in the words of an intelligent scientist, "The mind with its yearnings for and capabilities of religion is as much a part of nature as are the objects we may handle with our fingers; and the moral education of mankind has as much followed the lines of development, which the survival of the fittest demands, as has the physical advance of structural forms. Viewed in that light, the history of the human race, whether drawn from sacred or profane sources, is a history of the evolution and advance of moral sentiments." But they go on to call the manifestation of this growth in the Bible a "revelation," and the principle, unknown and inscrutable, which thus works for good or "makes for righteousness," they call "God"; and thus they retain their status among Christians as believers. This is a use of terms in a sense entirely different from their general acceptation. In this way, most rationalists believe as truly in God and revelation as they do; and I know honored men among Christians, who practically think as I do, who, by this accommodation of old phrases to their new ideas, are still accounted orthodox, and are held up to me as examples of the agreement of science and faith. The God of evolution is not God, as men in the Christian Church understand the name ; and, when they call the Bible a revelation, they believe it is the direct, authoritative, and final word of God, communicated in a miraculous manner to man,— not that it shows how men have gradually grown in religious knowledge, and is, therefore, a revelation to us. For the present, it seems wise and honest not to use the old phraseology, until men cease to misapprehend the intention and infer agreement with their own supernatural ideas. In this sense, the Unitarian use of the terms, "Our Lord and

Saviour, Jesus Christ," " Our Divine Master," while they utterly deny his deity and atonement in the orthodox sense, appears inconsistent and injurious to the progress of the demolition of superstition.

True freedom of speech will not be attained until men can be permitted to express their ideas about God as freely as their notions about geology. The First Cause is as legitimate an object of research as is electricity. The loftiest intellects of this age, who have gained conceptions of the Infinite Power as far above the Hebrew notions of Jehovah as are their differing ideas about astronomy, are liable to prosecution by some anti-blasphemy club, composed of men who believe that God has revealed nothing about himself for eighteen hundred years, and who accept as final the ideas of deity entertained by men whose opinions upon almost every other subject they despise. In their minds, to agree with the ancients in any of their opinions about nature is to show an ignorance and stupidity that is beneath contempt; but to differ from the ancients in their estimate of the greatest of all mysteries is blasphemy.

To sum up, in a few words, the main truths I desire to impress, I would say: The Bible, like all other books, is the product of men's minds. All ideas about God and the various doctrines of religion are likewise the products of men's minds. There has never been a revelation by God to man of final truth, given directly and all at once, either by word or vision. But all human ideas of religion are the result of a progressive development of man's mind, in accordance with the laws of evolution which pervade the universe, through which all growth in nature and all progress in man are promoted by the working of what men variously call "the inscrutable force," "eternal matter," "the great first cause," "the eternal and infinite spirit," "*the Almighty God.*"

PRAYER.

If all events are the effects of preceding causes, and God, the supreme power in the universe, acts only through natural laws, prayer in the form of petition is irrational and useless, unless it can be proved that prayer is a natural force.

Upon the orthodox ideas of God, petition to him to vary the succession of causes and effect is unreasonable and wrong. It is asking for blessing which involves suffering to others. The sailor who prays for a fair wind really asks that other sailors, equally deserving of prosperity, may have a head wind; and supposing that sailors pray, God is daily besought that the wind may blow from every point of the compass. How can he grant any of these petitions without injustice, even if the direction of the wind was not determined by natural laws which God has never interrupted? The flour merchant, praying for a rising market, asks God to do that which will make the laborer pay more for his bread. The laborer prays for cheap flour. How can God answer both prayers? The prosperity of one often means the adversity of another, the success of one the disappointment of his perhaps equally deserving fellow. How can a just God discriminate in the bestowal of answers? We narrate deliverance from shipwreck and accident in answer to prayer; but an honest consistency would oblige us to tell of shipwrecks in answer to prayer, and of misfortunes traceable to the following of "indications of Providence" succeeding prayer. Jesus had a wise conception of the limitations of prayer. The Lord's Prayer deals largely with desires for God's glory and man's moral improvement, its only material request being for daily bread, which every one would seem to have a natural right to possess. But it is more rational to work for it than to pray for it; and that this is the more effective course is proved by the popular proverb, "God helps those who help themselves."

Prayer is not only usually futile, but it is often injurious. It concentrates the mind upon itself and promotes selfishness. The calm of the evening subdues the throbbing brain of the business man; but, as he kneels by his bedside to pray, all the desires connected with his unfinished schemes are aroused, he often changes prayer into a renewal of his schemings, and, in utter forgetfulness of his purpose, calls back the trials and difficulties of the day, and his excited brain defers the approach of sleep. To some temperaments, the prayerless pillow brings the sweetest sleep. Prayer leads to trusting to God what should be sought by our own efforts. A landlady was overheard to pray imploringly that God would fill her house with boarders and bless her dog "Gypsy"; but she left her room and scolded so much at her servants that her boarders left her; and she stuffed her dog into an apoplectic condition. Prayer has been the resort of laziness, and has often paralyzed efforts and lost the attainment of desires, while the devout person was "waiting on the Lord" instead of using his best efforts for himself.

Prayer has an even chance of being answered or of failing, except that we usually pray for what is unlikely to happen. Most of the reputed answers to prayer are just this chance of having desire correspond to natural results. But there are some cases where prayer has really produced effects by its reflex influence: the will and faith of the devotee have affected the nervous organism and produced the desired result. The effect follows prayer to demons in Asia, to the Virgin and saints in Europe, and to Christ in America, and is therefore purely the action of physical laws. The shaking of the Joss-sticks in China, the whirling of the prayer-wheel in Burmah, the seven daily prostrations of the Mussulman, the counting of beads in Rome, and the prayer-meetings of Protestants, are alike in their measure of success or failure. Dr. Hammond, in the *International Review* for March, 1881, in a valuable article upon this subject, describes a cure effected by Croton water, labelled "Lourdes Water," after genuine Lourdes water labelled Croton had failed to produce effect, proving that the power lay in the imagination.

Perhaps, it may be found that prayer is sometimes effectual in another way. One or more persons sometimes "will" that another shall do certain things, and the acts are performed. This is believed to be a "psychological" influence; which only means that it is produced by a natural force that as yet we know but little of. In the *Nineteenth Century* for June, 1882, an article entitled "Thought Reading" gives most interesting facts of this character, with suggestions of explanation; and the editor adds a note containing a theory that "brain-waves" are produced by mental efforts, and sometimes affect others at a distance with a consciousness of the thought that caused them. Many visions, apparitions, and impressions would be explained by this theory, if it could be established. A man in a prayer-meeting felt an intense impulse to give a stranger five dollars. He did so with great diffidence, and learned that the stranger had been praying throughout the meeting for that sum, in order to bestow it upon a distressed person. This was narrated as an answer to prayer, and so it was. But, instead of its being the direct action of the Being invoked, is it not as well or better explained by the supposition that an intense desire may sometimes influence the mind of another person, or even affect natural forces in other ways, and thus produce the answer? If so, it is the feeling, and not the petition to God, which has brought about the result. Principal Dawson, in his latest work, "Facts and Fancies in Modern Science," says, "The bleat of the lamb will not only meet with response from the mother ewe, but will even exercise a physiological effect in promoting the secretion of milk in her udder. . . . In the case of animals there must be a certain relation between the one that prays and the one that answers." He argues for prayer to God, but such facts better illustrate the effects of desire upon natural resources.

When men become good and wise enough to "will" with benefit to themselves and others, we may find that the power of nature to produce results has also enlarged, and it may be found that the instinct of prayer was a dawning conception of a grand force to become available for man's use in a more developed state. As people meet now in a circle to "will" that a table shall move, the prayer-meeting will perhaps be succeeded by a gathering of intelligent persons who shall effectually "will" for results more useful to man, in certain directions where the possibility of success has been scientifically determined.

Meantime, the area of prayer will gradually be narrowed, as men learn to trace results to natural causes. They cease to ask God for things as fast as they learn nature's laws. No one prays that the sun may rise or that the seasons may change; and men are ceasing to pray for rain and wind and all other events, in proportion as they see that they are as inevitable as the sunrise, or else can be directed by their own knowledge.

But many rationalists, either from early habit or inherited impulse, while abandoning direct petition to God for specific material needs, delight in prayer as communion with the Power and Goodness which they perceive in nature, which they in a measure personify as God, and toward which or whom their spirit of thankfulness and wonder is outpoured. This it is not intended to criticise. The remarks made apply only to petitional prayer. Worship of God can do good only as it elevates the mental faculties to aspire toward a superior conception. Reverence for the powers of nature and an enthusiasm for the progress of humanity may produce as good effects upon the mind, and may lead to better results for the world.

MORALITY.

It is asked, If you take away the doctrine of the inspiration and infallible authority of the Bible, what foundation is left for morality? Those who ask the question believe that the Bible has created religion, instead of religion having made the Bible; and that morality springs from the ten commandments, instead of the commandments being the expression of human morality. Morality is the result of experience. That conduct which men have found to produce the best results has been inculcated by maxims which superstition ascribes to the finger of God upon stone tablets. The experience of ages is compressed into the Golden Rule, of which, when quoted by Christ, it is said, "For this is the law and the prophets" (Matt. vii., 12); and Moses gives the precept, "Thou shalt love thy neighbor as thyself." This rule and most of the maxims ascribed to Christ are found in writings centuries before he lived, and are the inheritance of the ages, needing no thunders of Sinai nor sufferings of Calvary to give them authority.

Thales, about 600 B.C., said, "Avoid doing what you would blame others for doing."

Pittacus, one of the seven wise men of Greece, about 570 B.C., said, "Avoid doing that to your neighbor which you would take amiss if he did it to you."

Confucius, the Chinese sage, 500 B.C., said: "What you do not want done to yourself do not do to others."

To one who has been accustomed to regard Jesus as the author of our present morality, it is instructive to read the maxims of the ancient philosophers of Greece and Rome and the teachers of Persia and India. Jesus summarized the morality of the past. If the Golden Rule be expressed in these words, Whatsoever ye would that men should do to you and yours, do ye even so to them and theirs, it seems impossible to imagine a relation in life to which it would not apply sufficient guidance and restraint. It teaches us to treat a man and his wife, sister, daughter, house, property, cow, dog, as we feel it would be right that a man should treat us and ours, and to set the example in speech, dress, and behavior we wish him to set. By this simple rule, we are thrown upon our conscience, and are relieved of all the burden of an immense code of maxims, which by their conflicting and unbending letter often destroy the spirit of morality. Education, which secures an enlightened conscience, will enable men to apply this rule rightly; and morality will not only stand, but grow purer and gain in universality, even though the Bible takes its rightful place among human compilations of man's deeds and thoughts. As Christ delivered his disciples from a yoke of ceremonials, which neither they nor their fathers "were able to bear," so modern criticism delivers men from the bondage of a multitude of rules which they call the word of God, but habitually violate, and leaves them with this grand "law of love" as the simple but effective guide.

The liberty which the Golden Rule gives is well expressed in the words of Herbert Spencer, in "Social Statics": "Every man has freedom to do all that he will, provided he infringes not the equal freedom of any other man"; and its restraints may be summed up in the words of Lecky, in his "History of European Morals": "Man must abstain from whatever injures happiness or degrades character."

Men will be more moral when they learn that morality does not rest for its authority upon arbitrary edicts thundered from the skies, but that its foundation is the experience of mankind as to what is best for man. Now, some men abstain from evil because they say God forbids it, or they do good because it is commanded so to do; but, when they learn to choose the good for its own sake, they will lose the sense of bondage which imbues virtue with the idea of self-sacrifice, and they will find, as Herbert Spencer says in the "Data of Ethics," that "the good is universally the pleasurable. Conduct is good or bad as its results to self or others is pleasurable or painful: the need for commandments from God disappears." He also remarks: "In the improved state of society there will be less self-sacrifice in helping others, and it will become pleasure. . . . Great miseries are caused by persevering in actions repugnant to the sensations, and neglecting actions which the sensations prompt."

We may with hope look forward to a day when men will instinctively and from pleasurable motives "refuse the evil and choose the good," though this will be attained to neither by eating "butter and honey" (Isaiah vii., 15) nor by slavish obedience, but by enlightened study of the laws of man's nature. But men are not yet all susceptible of control by moral suasion or "the enthusiasm of humanity"; and other restraints and impulses may still be necessary, as the "edicts of God" have been in the past. Morality must become approved to self-interest as well as to benevolence. Men must realize that it "pays better" to be good, but "the prosperity of the wicked" now weakens this conviction. Some indeed see but little advancement in the goodness of mankind, and are disposed to agree with Buckle that man only improves intellectually, not morally. A great impetus has been given to improvement in every other department of life, but some think there is not a corresponding advancement in morals. Even in the Church, where morality is believed to have made its highest progress, frailty is apparent. The large number of defaulters who have been "pillars of the Church" has excited much comment, and a good Christian lately remarked that he never had trusted implicitly in a religious man without being swindled.

As new forces have been discovered and applied by science and invention to the material use of man, may not a new motive be produced, which will give an impetus to the moral advancement of the human race?

In the past, the fear of God has been supposed to be the chief deterrent from the commission of evil acts; but experience proves that men are now only slightly influenced by the idea of the displeasure of God, and consequent future punishment. The scepticism of intelligence and the indefinite distance of the fulfilment of the threat alike make these motives ineffectual in restraining the accomplishment of present desires by improper means. The other great controlling motive against crime is the fear of the written and unwritten laws of man, but concealment makes these so often inoperative that their power as a deterrent is greatly modified. Not only is this evidenced among criminal classes, but in all the departments of business and social life, and even in Church and State, we continually see the futility of all known means of restraint to prevent deception and unfairness. The fear of God apparently exercises but little restraint, and the difficulty of detection and conviction abrogates the fear of man. Sir William Harcourt, when introducing the bill for the repression of crime in Ireland, said, " The mainspring of crime is the expectation of impunity." The telegraph, railroad, and detective police have done much to lessen the security of criminals ; but we need to find a way in which evidence can be secured, of so positive a character that concealment of wrong-doing shall be impossible, which, without resort to the old tortures of the Inquisition, shall extort the truth from witnesses or criminals, and prevent them from obtaining the shelter of " I don't know."

The researches of scientists have given plausibility, if not probability, to the theory that all mental action produces a permanent organic impression. As the phonograph registers sound by dents in the tinfoil, so mental consciousness may produce an ineffaceable record upon the organism of the brain ; and, as the phonograph is made to repeat what has been stamped upon its cylinder, so, under certain conditions, may the tablet of the brain give out its inscriptions. When read by the owner of the brain, the act is called " memory." Many occurrences are not thought of for years, until, under some intense mental excitement,—as in the act of drowning, the strife of battle, or at sudden alarm,—the mind becomes cognizant of certain records which these past events have made upon the brain. But it has been demonstrated that occasionally the records of the brain are read by others. Instances of this occur in what is known as second-sight, mind-reading, and clairvoyance; and it is beyond dispute that many persons have been able to discern the present thoughts and past history of others. The following case is mentioned in Fairfield's "Ten Years with Spiritual Mediums": Heinrich Zschokke, the Swiss poet and statesman, remarks, in his autobiography, that it has frequently been given to him, on his first interview with a stranger, to see the man's life passing before him like a dream. When dining with a friend at the hotel at Waldshut, a stranger entered into argument with him. Zschokke turned to the stranger, and at that moment he says, "The man's life passed before me; and I offered to tell him the various events of his past, if he would but frankly confess whether I was correct." He assented, and Zschokke proceeded with the narrative, from his student life to his later career, including a liberty he had once taken with the strong-box of his principal, describing the room and the black box on the table and the manner of its perpetration. The stranger was astounded, but frankly confessed the exactness and accuracy of the story. Numerous instances of this sort are well accredited, and even impressions made upon the eye without affecting consciousness have yet been so recorded upon the organism as to be legible to the mind-reader or clairvoyant.

Some writers, such as Blavatsky in "Isis Unveiled," go so far as to claim that all things that occur "are recorded on the tablet of the unseen universe. The adept can read and know all."

Superstition attributes this power to supernatural agency; but science suggests that there is a subtle condition of the faculties, as yet undefinable, in which the ability exists of becoming conscious of the brain records of others.

If this power of mind-reading is a physical trait, may it not, with advancing knowledge, be more clearly traced to its sources, and, as a result, may not its cultivation be possible, and thus certain persons be so trained as to be able to discern all the mental record of other persons? In time, this faculty might be widespread, so that one man could read another as he reads a book. What would be the effect of this upon crime? If the power of concealment is now the chief promoter of sin, will not the absolute certainty of exposure and conviction be the most repressive force that can be conceived of? If a man knows that the moment he meets another his record will be read, will not fraud, lying, theft, and murder be generally abandoned, simply because in most cases they would fail to attain their objects? This would either be the result, or else society would be so demoralized by the universal evidences of sin as to cease to reprobate or punish evil, and a moral degeneracy would everywhere prevail. But moral laws are now so well based upon natural necessities that there is little fear of this result.

The mere possibility of developing this faculty of mind-reading, and the consideration of the results which would flow from it, should excite great interest in the study of psychology; and if, through its researches, this power is secured to a reliable extent, we may see society regenerated by the fear of man.

Spencer says, "Not by authority is your sway to be obtained, neither by reasoning, but by inducement." When doing wrong invariably ceases "to pay," men will cease to do evil and learn to do well.

Buckle says, "The moral actions of men are not the product of their volition, but of their antecedents." And Herbert Spencer remarks, "All evil results from the non-adaptation of constitution to conditions." With a more enlightened understanding of the laws of heredity and a more rational and universal system of education, we shall find the tendency to crime diminishing. In the last forty years, criminal convictions in England have decreased fully one-half, while church attendance has declined. It is therefore not religion that has wrought the reform; but it may fairly be traced to intelligence, as manifested in the affairs of physical, mental, social, and industrial life. Were we wise enough, we could see that a man's ancestry, organism, and surroundings have made it necessary that he should act and think as he does, and that neither the "influence of the Spirit" nor his own free will are the true motive causes of his conduct. If this is true, eternal punishment for one's own sins is hardly just, even though some may praise God's justice in tormenting forever men born in this century, because Adam was immoral and they inherited his nature. It also encourages us to seek the moral improvement of man through material causes, instead of relying upon supernatural influences. Work and not prayer must be our instrument of reform. Pythagoras divides virtue into two branches,—to seek truth and to do good. The truth is to be sought through the study of the laws of nature, especially of those relating to man ; and good is to be done through efforts to improve the terrestrial condition of man. Men need to learn that truth is not only to be found in the Bible and through an imagined rapturous intercourse of the mind with Deity, and that good does not consist chiefly in church-going, psalm-singing, and saving men's souls.

One may worship the Good and serve the True, even if he does not personify them as God and

Christ. The differences in the beliefs of good men are rather matters of definition than questions of fact. Men may be equally devoted to the welfare of others, though one calls it "working for Christ," and another "helping man."

The moral maxims of the New Testament have in many instances become obsolete, and the development of society is evolving new rules of conduct. Another table of commandments is in preparation, and will be given to men by God as truly as were the first. But they will very likely find utterance in the "resolutions" of a convention, composed of the wisest and best men of the world. Perhaps the new table will embrace such laws as these :—

Thou shalt give women equal rights with men.

Thou shalt give a fair day's pay for a fair day's work, and the laborers shall share with the capitalists the profits of their enterprises.

Thou shalt not protect one industry at the expense of another, and thou shalt not refuse free trade with other nations.

Thou shalt tax all property alike, religious or secular.

Thou shalt not give religious instruction in public schools, nor force any to pay for the support of religious practices which they do not approve.

Thou shalt not advance the price of merchandise by "corners."

Thou shalt lay up treasure upon earth, but shalt use it for the benefit of man.

Many rationalists do not accept this "utilitarian" scheme of morals, which rests upon experience and results ; but, with the transcendentalists, they believe that man possesses innate ideas or intuitions, which are above the senses, telling what is right and just, without regard to consequences as a motive for action. Lecky, Theodore Parker, and the Concord philosophers are among the expounders of this view.

It is perhaps the greatest question now before the thinker ; for the grandest problem of life is how to make men better and happier, and the way in which moral ideas are gained is an essential factor in the solution.

THE FUTURE.

BIBLICAL scholars are generally agreed that there is no indisputable evidence in the earlier books of the Old Testament that the doctrine of the immortality of the soul and a future life was known to the Jews of those days. It is an idea which gradually gained currency among philosophers, and was emphasized by Jesus and the apostles. It was not revealed by them, for it was believed before their day. If, when it was made known, it was received by way of direct revelation from God, it may rightly be asked why God, who talked with men, kept such needful knowledge carefully concealed for so many ages, and let his friends, the men after his own heart, live and die in ignorance of so important a truth, virtually deceiving them as to the facts of their existence. But the late attainment of the idea is explained, if we accept the theory that it is a higher intellectual conception than the earlier races of men were capable of exercising, and has been developed from the advancing mind of man. As to the proof of its truth, we must say that there is none beyond the fact of its belief: there is no evidence of a future life that will bear the test of examination ; but there are strong analogies in nature and an intense yearning in man which stimulate the *hope* that death does not end all. Hamlet's soliloquy expresses this argument. The pictures of heaven given in the New Testament are the fond imaginations of the writers of that age, and are not acceptable to the present generation, who have no more delight in the prospect of white robes and harps, and the song of Moses and the Lamb, than in the land of Watts' conception, "where congregations ne'er break up and Sabbaths have no end." Each age and clime makes heaven for itself. The modern authoress changes the harp into a piano; the tropical negro looks to a cool, shady grove; and the Esquimaux believes in a land of sunshine. These imaginations may do no harm, and may even be beneficial and comforting, if kept in the right place; but when they exalt the world to come over this world, as the rightful object of our concern, they are hurtful. The Bible teaches that this world is condemned of God on account of the sin of the man he made; and his long-suffering patience is gathering out a few favored elect ones to dwell in a new heaven and new earth, when he has destroyed the present abode of man and the vast majority of its inhabitants. As in the days of Noah, so it is to be at the coming of the Lord. Consistent Christians, therefore, "love not the world, neither the things that are in the world," and ignore all attempts to improve what God has cursed, which cannot be regenerated by any efforts of man. They teach that Christians should not engage in politics, nor hold office, nor seek wealth, nor crave pleasure; but, with loins girded and lamps trimmed and burning, should wait for their Lord. The majority of Christians, however, are not of this mind, and believe in making the best of both worlds, though any candid reader of the New Testament must see that they are a different order of Christians from the original sect, and have virtually evolved a new religion to suit the times.

The apostles and early Christians were looking for the speedy return of Christ, and therefore taught contempt of the world. Their hope being false, as is that of those who now wait for his appearance, their conclusions are therefore wrong. A good old man, who spent his days in prayer and tract distribution, was admiring the noble ship in which I was about to embark on a voyage around the world. "Yes," I said, "we hope to have some good times in her."

"Ah, my dear brother," said he, "we can't take any pleasure in this world that has crucified our Lord."

His view of life was similar to that of the "dear brother" who shut his eyes in the cars, lest the beauties of this world should distract his thoughts from Christ and the age to come. They considered inventions and arts as man's effort to improve what God had condemned. Though Christians generally may now disavow these pietistic views, they cannot deny their Scripturalness; and consistency should lead them to follow them, or else admit that the New Testament is not their infallible guide. These views of the future life, as being so immeasurably the object of our concern, discourage efforts for the increase of knowledge and invention or the improvement of the material condition of man, the saving of his soul being all that is worth attention, since the world and all in it is to be burned up. Some writers maintain that any hope of immortality is injurious, as necessarily distracting thought and effort from the present life; but it is not clear that this must be so, if it is recognized as only a hope, the realization of which is not so definite as to warrant the engrossment of the faculties in its contemplation. If we make the best of this world, when another comes we shall find we have made the best possible preparation for it. Spinoza says, "The proper study of a wise man is not how to die, but how to live."

If we never awake from our dreamless sleep, we shall never know our loss. Life is a burden to most people. Their happiest moment is when they are just falling into sleep; and they usually awake with a sigh, as the consciousness of another day's care comes to the mind. Some writer has said man's happiest hours are those which he passes in childhood and in sleep. Why, then, should eternal sleep be so dreaded? The rational mind must reject the idea of a perfect future state, for there must ever be progress upward. Life must therefore always be in some sense a struggle; and, though ambition prompts the desire to engage in it, yet the weary laborer need not shudder at the thought of eternal unconscious rest, and may "sink to sleep" more peacefully than though agitated with thoughts of angels and unwonted glories.

But, if this hope has grown in man as his intelligence has increased, it has been founded upon fact or has been useful. If it is not true, when it ceases to be useful, it will be discarded; and, if it is true, the demand which man's mind now makes for evidence, without which no belief can much longer exist, will be met by proof, which his advancing powers will elicit from nature. If there is any light to be gained on this subject from the phenomena of "Spiritualism," it will in time be made plain. Immortality is one of the mysteries which we may not deny, but which as yet we do not know. If it cannot be positively denied, and there is therefore a possibility of its truth, it is not irrational to hope for it.

The aim of life should therefore be to assist in the subjection of the laws of nature to man's use, and to improve the moral, intellectual, and social condition of man. Instead of endeavoring to convert men to a belief in theories which will make them happy in a hereafter, of which we know nothing and which men through the ages have conceived of differently, according to their own temperaments, we should aid the progress, which history shows has slowly but surely been going on, of making man the master of this world. The application of steam, gas, electricity, and some only suspected forces to the comfort and power of man, offers an unbounded field to the man of science or the practical mechanic; while the philosopher and theologian can turn their devotion and credulity from the myths of darker ages to the discovery of psychological laws, which, hinted to us in the phenomena of "Spiritualism," suggest a vast enlargement in the range of man's intellectual powers. They can study the problem of moral restraint without the supposition of divine edicts, the methods of raising the profits of labor to a more just proportion to those of capital, the abolition of the selfish, demoralizing, and partial laws of so-called "protection of industry," which makes each nation the commercial enemy of every other, and robs its many citizens for the benefit of the few, and, by the promotion of free trade and the intercourse of reciprocal commerce all over the world, develop the bonds of peace, which will forever chain the demon of war and bind all men into a universal brotherhood. The Christian, instead of being "a man of one book," and that a compilation of the traditions of a credulous age, will become a student of the volumes of nature, and learning its facts will discover its laws. Winwood Reade in "The Martyrdom of Man" says: "There is a great enterprise in which men have always unconsciously been engaged, but which they will pursue with method as an avocation and an art, which they will devoutly adopt as a religious faith, as soon as they realize its glory. It is the conquest of the planet on which we dwell, the destruction or domestication of the savage forces by which we are tormented and enslaved." He says, when men made fire serve them, the first victory was won. "But we can conquer Nature only by obeying her laws, and we must first learn what they are."

If the Bible predictions as to the world's future are to be classed with the innumerable myths and legends that pervade the literature of all people, what does Science teach us? She knows nothing of the future save what is taught by the analogy of the facts of the past. What has been will be: that is all that she can say. She finds in the past a slow, painful process of improvement going on in all animate Nature; and she assumes that it will go on, and things that improve forever must in time approach perfection. But she finds evidences of a limit to the existence of worlds, and sees a possibility of such changes in condition as to lead to the extinction of all life on this globe, though vast ages must elapse before this result could ensue from the orderly progression of causes which have worked in the past.

The pre-millennial scheme of the speedy advent of Christ to miraculously perfect the earth, after destroying the evil men in it, and then in a thousand years burning the world itself up, and the post-millennial theory of the gradual but not far distant conversion of the world to Christianity, and a thousand years of blessedness followed by the appearance of Christ to destroy the world, find no support from the records of what has been. No one can say it may not be so, but there are the best of reasons for believing it will not be so. God has never told us it would be thus; and the story which many believe came from God is so differently interpreted under "the infallible guidance of the Holy Ghost," by those to whom the revelation is supposed to have been given, that no two men can agree as to the details of fulfilment; and as to the event of greatest concern, the appearance of Christ, believers in his coming are at least a thousand years apart in their reckonings. When God gives us a revelation, he will be likely to tell us something; but a tale of war-horses, and trumpets, and vials of wrath, and beasts, which most learned men tell us mean great events of past history, but disagree as to what they are, the beast being Antiochus Epiphanes, or Nero, or the Pope, or the Church of Rome, or Louis Napoleon,—and which other equally wise men declare refer to events that have not yet happened, the beast being a wicked ruler yet to appear,—this tale seems to a rational mind to be more probably the poetic imagining of the religious prophets of a less enlightened age than the present, than the instruction from God as to what man is to expect. It is impossible that the God which the nineteenth century can alone conceive of should *reveal* what is unintelligible. A noted orthodox theologian has said, "The study of the Book of Revelation either finds or leaves a man crazy"; and yet at its beginning the Holy Ghost says, "Blessed is he that readeth and they that hear the words of the prophecy."

If things are to go on, what then may we expect? We are warranted in believing that the forces of nature will become the servants of man. Time and space will be almost annihilated by aerial flight, talking on beams of light, electric and pneumatic despatches, and other modes of movement and communication. New motive powers and machinery will abolish the *curse* of labor. Chemistry will create cheap food. Social science will distribute wealth more equally, banish land monopolies, let producers get a greater benefit than they now do in comparison with the gains of the capitalist. Muscle, and brains, and money will share results in more equitable proportions. But what of sin? Of what use is all this, while it may yet be said, "Only man is vile"? History certainly shows that man is less vile than he was once; and, if he has improved, we are warranted in hoping he will "go on unto perfection." The telegraph, the newspaper, and the high moral sentiment which is the standard of society now, bring to notice a multitude of crimes that in old times would not have gained publicity, both from the lack of facilities for publication and the prevailing lax morality which would have ignored them. These increased exhibits of sin cause some to mourn over the degeneracy of the times, and to sigh for a return of the good old days. If they will read the histories of those days, they will find cause for gratitude that they do not date their births any earlier. Governments, all will admit, have improved; and, as laws are the expressions of the wills of the governed, it follows that men collectively, and therefore individually, have improved. If society is better, man is better. The social conditions of the Middle Ages, or the Roman Empire, or the days of Abraham were morally inferior to those of to-day; and though, individually, man's morality does not seem to have kept pace with the material improvement of his circumstances, it must be admitted that it has advanced, and therefore probably will advance.

Lewes in "Problems of Life and Mind" says: "Among the many strange servilities mistaken for pieties, one of the least lovely is that which hopes to flatter God by despising the world and vilifying human nature. The author of creation is the only author who is supposed to be flattered by the lavish assurance that his works are imbecile." While men insist on styling themselves vile worms of the dust, they not only insult the God who they believe made them, but they retard the progress of man.

Man's conception of Deity is the evidence of the aspiration of his nature and of the goal toward which his energies and desires are directed. The qualities and powers which men have most desired to attain to, they have attributed to God; and the progress of humanity in each age is toward the character and ability of its God. Man's thought of God, therefore, becomes a prophecy of his own destiny, and in ages to come man may rise to the possession of the attributes of his present God. What intimations we already have of this,—travel by steam, aerial voyages, talking by telegraph, telephone and photophone, listening with the microphone! Time and space are being annihilated by these inventions, which convey a suggestion of the omnipresence of man.

The phenomena of mind-reading, clairvoyance, and second sight, may be the germs of a rising ability which may increase to a capacity for what seems to us infinite knowledge, and man will become omniscient.

The application of chemistry to the arts, of mechanical invention to manufactures, of electricity, animal magnetism, will-power, and other physical and psychic forces to the general necessities of men, give us a foreshadowing of a future omnipotence.

When man thus becomes relatively omnipresent, omniscient, and omnipotent, and a corresponding moral advance and "love to man" are gained, his present ideal of God will be in a great measure realized; and the true "coming of the Lord" to earth, for which all ages have hoped and waited, will become a fact.

THE CHURCH AND ITS WORK.

WE find a world-wide institution, known among Christians as the Church, which may be defined as the association of people for the exercise of religious emotions. It has its church buildings, temples, mosques, and schools, ministers, priests, and teachers. Some rationalists attack this institution, charge it with every crime against humanity and obstruction of its advancement, and demand its overthrow and destruction. The evolutionist must see that such a course is highly irrational; for so universal an organization must have been founded upon the necessities of man's nature, and has doubtless contributed to its development. Its vast system, if the analogy of nature's workings is to be followed, will not be destroyed, but will become the promoter of better things. The change is perceptibly going on, and is loudly lamented by many adherents. Church attendance is falling off, ministers say, "because men are growing worldly and wicked"; others say, "because people are becoming too intelligent to be interested in ministers' preaching." Ministers are being expelled from the churches for "heresy," and others are preaching "qualified views," as far as they dare. The number of ministers is proportionably lessening, because the education of the times prevents young men from putting upon their intellects the yoke of bondage prescribed by the old creeds of the Churches, and it is foreseen that the only prospect which a thinking man has before him in the ministry is quarrelling and separation. If he preaches the old theology, unless he is a genius or a mountebank, he will be considered dull, and the church will dismiss him for not filling the pews and making the church pay; and if he preaches on the topics of the times and shows advancing ideas about Moses and Joshua, although he draws a full house, some conscientious hearers will stir up disaffection, which will make him glad to accept "a providential call to a wider sphere of usefulness."

Attendants upon churches wonder why it is they are so listless and sleepy, more interested in bonnets than in the sermon; why the children cry because they have to go "to that horrid church"; why they can listen with breathless interest on a week-day evening for two whole hours to their bright minister's lecture about his "Trip to California," and on Sunday his "gifted" long prayer of fifteen minutes excites only a responsive snore, and his forty-five minutes' exposition of Jacob "watering stock," as Ingersoll expresses it, or Simon Peter catching fish, produces yawns. Why is it, men ask, that the press and the platform are so popular, while the pulpit is losing power? This is the true answer : the first treat of live facts, the last deals with dead and dying fiction. Only what is real can long enchain men's attention in this age. Many come out of church feeling, and perhaps saying, "There is something wrong about this : it does not satisfy one's cravings, it is not in the line of nature, something must be done to make preaching interesting." The change to be made is to substitute the true for the false. Destroy the churches? No, let them be the grand lecture rooms, enforcing morality, humanity, and education by exposition of the glorious and fast revealing facts of nature, upon which alone they rest, and which supply the only lasting incentive to their culture. Let Sunday be the great day of mental instruction and elevating diversion to the toiling millions, in Sunday-schools, churches, libraries, art galleries, fields, and woods. We need preachers and teachers all the more, lest the new-found liberty degenerate into license, as it always does with some natures, who have known only the restraints of law. Let radicals not be too eager to overthrow existing institutions ; let them rather work in nature's way of growth, till the shackles burst by the full development of what they confine. The "crimes of Christianity" are the expression of the ignorant passions of the dark ages ; and, as J. W. Chadwick has remarked, if men had not persecuted through the power of the Church, the same forces would have produced something equally bad. Give the credit that is due to Christianity, and preserve all that is helpful to man in its creed and organization. All that is good and elevating in the life of Jesus is the heritage of man: let us profit still by its benign influence, and, while we "prove all things, hold fast that which is good."

The Church is changing in accord with the spirit of the age. As interest and belief in doctrines subside, the church organization becomes useful in social and benevolent schemes. Parties, literary and musical entertainments, picnics and fairs, cause churches to be valued by many as religious fun-clubs, and a decreased interest in souls gives larger scope for action to increase the temporal welfare of men.

What would Jesus think of the Church, if he came to earth again as a man? and what would the churches think of him? Is there a pulpit in a fashionable church where he would be invited to preach? If he stood at the church door and said to the rich deacon, as he came toward the carriage, "Sell all that thou hast and give to the poor, and come follow me," would not the deacon call for a policeman?

Many intelligent and scholarly ministers, who are outgrowing belief in the Calvinistic creeds to which they are officially committed, realize that these dogmas are driving from the Church men whose practical sympathies and purposes are entirely in accord with their own. To save such persons to the Church, the invitation to the Lord's Supper is made so broad that few need to turn their backs on it. One is told that, if he only can profess "loyalty to Jesus," he may reserve all opinions about evangelical doctrines. An agnostic, who denies all that is supernatural in the records of the life of Jesus, is admitted to membership in a Congregational church; and one who in honest consistency feels obliged to renounce membership is told that he should have remained inside, and helped to bring the Church to the rational position toward which it is slowly moving. At present men who feel obliged to antagonize erroneous creeds are placed in a false position, as apparently opposed to the practical morality of Christianity. When the churches disavow the false dogmas with which goodness has become entrusted, their practical aims and work will be assisted by many who now feel their only consistent standing-place is outside the Church.

The charity and missionary organizations of the Church must be preserved, and their working improved in method and enlarged in scope. Foreign missions are doing a great educational work, and are yearly tending toward a larger interest in the establishment of schools and colleges than in the propagation of theologies. A leader in foreign mission efforts told me, with an injunction of secrecy, that he was much less interested than formerly in the society of which he was a manager, because in their policy the salvation of souls was becoming more and more secondary to the education of the mind. We shall some day see these agencies devoted solely to spreading moral and physical knowledge among savages and ignorant nations, and then earnestly supported by rationalists. The wholesale denunciation of missionaries is unjust. I have visited numbers of mission stations, and never saw one where there was not an apparent influence for good nor where the workers were not faithful and earnest people. The religion they teach is certainly better than the one it displaces, and the dogmas of theology are not made as prominent as they are at home. When they are entirely dropped from the teaching, and missionary societies become educational societies wholly, they will demand and receive the support of all intelligent men.

Those who still believe in the story of the Tower of Babel must be puzzled, as I used to be, to explain how God should have caused the existence of the greatest obstacle to the spread of knowledge,—the diversity of languages. Since learning that this story is the myth of an ignorant people, I am relieved from the necessity of believing that God, who "desires all men to repent and come to the knowledge of the truth," has been the greatest enemy of foreign missions.

Theological seminaries at present are mainly institutions where men are taught how to maintain preconceived theories formulated by their ancestors. The education thus given is one-sided, for fact is warped to conform to theory. The language of the Bible is made to conform to the desired notion by taking it literally, figuratively, or spiritually, as best suits the requirement. I am convinced that the peculiar difficulty attending the settlement of theological discussions is owing to the habit of mind which is formed by the custom of spiritualizing the meaning of Scripture words, when it helps an argument to do so. It creates an unconscious tendency to an unfair use of language in controversy. A Congregational minister tells me that his roommate at Andover Seminary felt unable to assent to the creed. The professor said, "Oh, you can subscribe to it as we all do, in the sense which the words mean in your own mind." The necessity for such warping of mind and conscience must be injurious to intellect and heart.

But the theological seminary is not to be discarded. It may become the greatest help and the grandest power. Workers in every field of science are gathering facts, each in his own special department; and the need of a generalization of results is most apparent. The varied facts must be gathered, harmonized, and arranged in systems and philosophies, and the theological seminary is the place to do it. Instead of an exclusive study of Hebrew religion, upon the false assumption that this alone is revealed by God and all others are inventions of men, a studious comparison of all religions will be made, and the development of the religious idea in man will be traced and followed out scientifically, showing its past connections and suggesting its future resolution into one universal creed. Instead of dismissing diversity of language by a summary reference to Babel, a comparative study of ancient languages will throw light upon the growth of speech and give indications of the methods to secure a universal language. Instead of the vain effort to reconcile Genesis and science, the views of the Hebrews about nature will only have an antiquarian interest, and religion will cease to oppose all knowledge that conflicts with the theology of the Jews. Then, with unbiassed mind, the newly revealed facts of nature can be studied with reference to their relation to the infinite first cause. Political economy and many branches of social science could here find a proper nursery. In fact, there will be no end to the sphere of usefulness opened when the theological seminary shall be changed into the scientific theorizing seminary.

Christian institutions, therefore, are to be enlarged in scope, even though the names be not changed. We, who desire to be in active accord and harmony with all efforts for the welfare of man, call upon the many ministers who by the light of science have discovered the falsity of the creeds they are bound to, asking them boldly to instruct their people in the truths revealed by the evolution philosophy and modern Biblical criticism, that they may cease to shun and despise good and intelligent men who have learned that the Bible is a human compilation of scattered and fragmentary Hebrew literature, and that God has never acted save through natural laws. When these senseless prejudices, survivals of paganism and ignorance, are removed, all who love their fellow-men and whose religion is to do good can unite in the practical worship of the Church universal.

THE DECLINE OF THE MINISTRY.

FROM many quarters arise complaints that the number of young men in preparation for the ministry is continually lessening. In England, it is said that the learning of Oxford and Cambridge diverts their graduates from the Church; and in America, we are told, the physics of the colleges indisposes students from the pursuit of metaphysics in theological seminaries. It appears that we are called to consider the prospect of an important decline in the supply of ministers, and it is therefore timely to reflect upon its causes and probable results.

Those who habitually sneer at the ministerial profession, and devote themselves to cataloguing and portraying its crimes, do injustice to a body of men who are unsurpassed in excellence of character, social virtue, and intellectual culture, and who in the past have been eminent in influences for good. What may seem to us at present injurious in their methods may have been beneficial in former conditions of the general knowledge and social habits of the people. They have been the trusted counsellors of the young, the consolers of the afflicted, the comforters of the aged, the promoters of all charitable effort, and their practical influence of late years has usually been on the side of human advancement, except where the maintenance of dogma has in some cases interfered. But the fact remains that their number is becoming proportionally less.

The first and most immediate result of a scarcity of ministers will be the decline of sectarianism. This will proceed from two causes. First, Baptist, Methodist, and Congregational churches in small villages will be led by economical reasons to unite. Universalists and Unitarians will often, from the same motives, coalesce; and even Episcopalians may consent to embrace outsiders in their fold, though not likely to merge their organization in those of other sects. The second influence is the same that causes the scarcity of ministers,—the growth of knowledge that destroys belief in the dogmas of supernaturalism. This affects minister and people alike, leading to less insistence upon what are considered non-essentials, and creating a necessity for union upon the central truths vital to the existence of the Christian system, in order to resist the inroads of the hosts of rationalism. A continuation of this process, now perceptibly progressing, leads logically to a future existence of one Protestant Church united in a struggle for existence.

Some significant instances of this spread of modern ideas among theologians will be useful in illustration of the tendency of the Church toward liberal views that favor the union of sects. A free thinker yielded to the urgent desire of his friends that he should confer with an eminent doctor of divinity, thoroughly versed in science and philosophy, and competent to refute modern scepticism. With trepidation, he entered the doctor's house; but the genial theologian put him at ease, and, instead of criticising scepticism, proceeded to utter such sentiments as these: "When the Reformation came, a substitute was needed for the infallible Church of Rome as a rallying point and centre of faith; and the disconnected and fragmentary literature of the Hebrews was elevated into an infallible book. This Bibliolatry must be destroyed. Men need to learn that the Bible is not a book, and to judge of its contents as other writings are studied. Intolerance and bigotry are founded upon this false estimate of the authority of the Scriptures. I reject the supernatural entirely. I think something occurred which made the Bible writers think they saw what they described; but, if the events occurred, they were in harmony with natural law." The doctor went on to make light of the dogma of eternal punishment, and to deprecate the abuse which Christians shower upon unbelievers whose reasons they either lack courage or intelligence to examine. He said, "The Church is gradually coming to these views upon inspiration and Calvinistic dogma; and you should remain in the Church, and help those of us who are trying to bring her to a rational position, instead of attacking it from outside, where you have but little influence."

The free thinker said, " Do I understand that you have no criticism to make upon my doctrinal position, but only upon my attitude in leaving the Church and attacking its errors?"

" I do," the doctor replied. " You are substantially right, and the Church will some day stand where you do; but it will be a long time, and you do not want to associate with these infidels and low fellows, and throw away your influence."

" But," said the free thinker, "where are your honesty and consistency in remaining in an orthodox pulpit?"

" My Church has no creed," replied the doctor. " You could state your views to your pastor, and yet remain in association with the Church." He extolled the benefits of Christianity as a system, and pleaded for the necessity of its continuance as an organization with modified beliefs.

Another orthodox doctor of divinity was asked by a rationalist to give his views of the inspiration of the Bible. He replied as follows: "In the evolution of the human mind, the Greeks developed the greatest aptitude for art, the Romans for law, and the Hebrews for religion. As I accept a

Greek statue and Roman law, so I take the religious writings of the Hebrews. The authority of these writings is not in their origin, but in their merits; and I adopt only what appeals to my own consciousness as truth." Some remarks excited a question as to the doctor's "soundness" upon the Trinity and the deity of Christ, and he went on to say: " I gave up the doctrine of eternal punishment twenty years ago. I don't know that I am 'orthodox,' but such are my convictions. I do not state them in my pulpit, because the time has not yet come, and the people are not prepared for such utterances; but, if any one asks my opinions in private, I express them frankly."

Both these good men, upon prominent occasions, when they were reported widely by the press, made vehement denunciations of extreme rationalism, and said nothing against superstition. Thus, their status among the orthodox was preserved; and the heresy hunters, who already were on their tracks, were turned aside. Some may call them hypocrites, but they are not consciously insincere. They are most estimable men; but they have outgrown the system to which they are allied, and upon which their support and all that is to them pleasant in life depends. They are in advance of their people and their creeds; but they know they will be overtaken in time, and prudence suggests patience and accommodation to the changing age. Perhaps they also share somewhat in the considerate temper of another orthodox minister of high repute, who wrote to an unbelieving and critical correspondent: " I do without any concealment declare that I do not believe the whole Bible to be true; that there are human additions and interpolations; that, in fact, Robertson Smith is right in the view he takes. Must I say all I think to the weak and stupid public? for such it is. I never say anything I *don't* believe. I only act on Christ's own principle,—' I have many things to say unto you, but you cannot bear them now.' Yes, God is afraid of upsetting weak minds, if Christ echoed the divine view of things in that statement."

Men not in the ministry hesitate to enter a profession where such suppression of conviction is a necessary policy; but it is perhaps fortunate that many who are in it can conscientiously square opposed belief and profession, as they save themselves much distress, and may aid in the slow process by which nature usually acts in promoting the evolution of ideas. People may be led better by those a little ahead of them than by those far in advance. But, unless the host advances rapidly, near leaders will be scarce; for new men will not assume such equivocal positions.

The question then arises, How can we do without ministers? The chief offices of the ministry are in connection with marriages, funerals, visitations, sacraments, and church services. What substitutes can be employed? The civil magistrate can secure the marriage bond. The professional utterance at the side of the dead will either not be missed by the mourners, with whom each word at such times stirs up the fountains of grief, or it may be acceptably replaced by the simple tribute of a friend and comrade, who knew the departed as few ministers ever come to know their parishioners. Visitation of the sick can be more agreeably carried on by neighbors and friends, who now often deprive the invalid and themselves of the mutually beneficial expression of sympathy and acts of kindness, because that is considered the pastor's sphere. Sacraments, if continued, can be administered by laymen. Church attendance has too many social attractions to be given up; and, where a minister is lacking, the services might be conducted after this manner: A committee should be formed to control them, one of whom should in turn preside. The music could be indefinitely improved; and its sphere and character, as to words, tunes, and instruments, enlarged. Readings of scriptures from ancient and modern authors should be given by young people of both sexes who possess oratorical talent. If prayer is not outgrown, there will be always good brethren " gifted " in that respect, some of whom may even exercise the somnolent influence attending "the long prayer." But how can the sermon be replaced? By reading a printed discourse? By no means. Every congregation possesses thinking and cultured men with good utterance. Let these read original papers upon the themes they are most familiar with, the subject first being approved by the committee. Let there be one paper of half an hour's length at each service, and let a discussion follow for another half-hour in five-minute speeches. At the close, let the people linger for friendly greetings. Many advantages will be gained by this method. Each person's mind runs in certain directions and emphasizes particular truths, and one man's instructions must lack variety. How many churches have been bored by their minister's specialty! How many have got tired of the pre-millennial advent, election, free grace, eternal punishment, the sinfulness of the world, or praises of its progress, when one of these things has been lugged into every sermon for a year! Few men have the versatility to preach instructively to the same people continuously; or, at any rate, people are benefited by receiving truth from varied sources. What interest would be felt in each new speaker, and what attention would be given to the essay in anticipation of the discussion! The joys of church-going would still exist: the best clothes can be worn and seen; the invalid, the baby, the absent, can be inquired for; the newcomer can be observed; acquaintance can be made that otherwise would never be formed; differences healed by a shake of the hand in passing in the aisle or porch; and Augustus can exchange a word or glance with Mary Jane, which will make his step the lighter in the store and her carol the livelier in the house throughout the week. Perhaps, too, with the absence of the theologian, theology will disappear, and men will talk of what they *know* and of what concerns their present lives. Salary will be saved, and independent thought secured from men whose opinions are unbiassed by their pay.

If, then, the vicissitudes of time deprive us of ministers, we may still hope that beneficent nature will supply substitutes, and that progress and happiness will continue. We need not wait till the clerical race is extinct before these methods are tried. Any pastorless church might make the experiment, and, while saving the salary, leave one more available minister to supply the field. Some Liberals, in whom early habit has confirmed the church-going instinct, would be likely to resume church-going under such secular auspices.

THE CONSOLATIONS OF CHRISTIANITY.

It is often asserted that the unbeliever in Christianity is "without hope and without God in the world." He is supposed to have abandoned all sources of comfort in affliction, and to be destitute of joy and peace in his meditations and aspirations. Does observation show that the believer has an advantage over the unbeliever as to happiness? We not only claim that this is not the case, but that the rationalist has superior grounds for a glad and hopeful spirit.

The Christian religion fails to produce the results claimed for it. An intelligent physician states that he has witnessed more fear of death and more distress upon the death-bed among Christians than among unbelievers. He says he has never witnessed a painful death of an unbeliever. His explanation is that Christians contemplate the end of life and a future state more frequently, and the proofs are not strong enough to allay the fears that these meditations arouse. Every one can recall aged "saints" who have lived excellent lives and have always been devout and prayerful, yet who close their lives in gloom and despondency. One of the most notable Christian women, the wife of a Congregational deacon, lately died, after years of depression, in which she lamented her lack of assurance of salvation. Her son met the son of her pastor, and exclaimed, "My poor mother's life was made wretched by that infernal theology!" One whose especial gift was the utterance of words of consolation, and whose written words are often presented to mourners, while expressing resignation to his own trials, suffered greatly from depression of spirits, and was unable to deliver himself from continual brooding over his troubles. Many a saint of pious speech and unhappy life may be observed, and broken-hearted mourners whose words of submission are belied by their inconsolable grief. Several men of bright faith whom I have known, who could cast their cares upon Jesus and leave all the burden with him, were men of strong physique and sanguine temperament. Few more incongruous events remain in my memory than the visit of a minister of extraordinary physical strength, a sledge hammer preacher, and man of buoyant spirits, to a lady of most delicate constitution, but of the most exquisite and refined character and cultivation, and the distress he occasioned by the assertion that all her ailments and sorrows were owing to lack of "faith." It seems demonstrable that happiness in life is dependent upon health, inherited temperament, and one's surroundings, and that the theories of the Christian religion never triumph over an adverse combination of these particulars. Many think they get comfort from religion, because during the rest and contemplation of Sunday their spirits rise, and by night their "faith" is strong. But this often only lasts till Monday noon, by which time the cares of life have consumed their "joy in the Lord"; and they toil on for the rest of the week "bearing the cross," and saying, with heavy sighs, "Though he slay me, yet will I trust in him." It was not theology, but the physical recuperation gained by a day of rest that enlivened the mind.

Sorrow comes to all, and only time allays its affliction. Mourners grasp at alleviations, and try to gain comfort from the sentiments we see touchingly expressed in obituary notices in the newspapers. They try to find joy in the thought,—

> "There was in heaven an angel band
> That was not quite complete:
> God took our little Mary Ann
> To fill the vacant seat."

Or they seek peace in the submissive plaint,—

> "Dearest Tommy, thou hast left us,
> And thy loss we deeply feel;
> But 'tis God that has bereft us,
> He will all our sorrows heal."

But still the vacant chair, the little empty shoes, the absent laugh, and the lost endearing caress cause pangs of grief that only subside with the lapse of years.

It often only aggravates the affliction to be told that God has arbitrarily caused it, in chastening love or in judgment; for its need or justice is not perceived, and the spirit rebels against such severe treatment and fails to believe in its necessity. But where disaster is seen to be the result of natural law, that death comes in consequence of inherited or acquired weakness or by reason of man's imperfect knowledge, then we can bow to the inevitable, and resolve that our sad experience shall be a factor in producing a more rational life and a more eager pursuit of the laws of health and the conquest of disease.

But it is not only in affliction that the Christian claims superior consolation; he asserts that his hope of heaven sustains his spirits, and makes him endure present ills. Doubtless, many are cheered by these thoughts : but those who cannot entertain them find they have been delivered from a selfish conceit, that sought joy in an exceptional personal advantage, and ignored an inconceivable amount of woe to their friends and neighbors. If a person claims he has gained in happiness by renouncing evangelical religion, he is accused of arrogance, as implying that Christians are not happy. But he does not assert that they are not happy, but that they have no right to be so. No man of unselfish mind and tender sensibility can be happy in the assurance of salvation, when he knows that good and estimable people all around him are doomed to eternal damnation. If I take the liberty of expressing my personal sentiments, I shall doubtless echo the feeling of many others.

In the past, the doctrines of Calvinism have been a pall upon my joy. If I was happy, it was in spite of them; and often, after a period of delight in innocent recreation, an accusing conscience has reproached me with the inconsistency of mirth while the vast procession of human life was marching by to hell. It was not enough that I was saved: I wanted my equally good friends to be saved also. But they would not believe the doctrines; and, therefore, nothing remained to them but "a fearful looking for of judgment and fiery indignation." God, of his own free will, had elected me to be saved and had left them to perish,— not that I was any better than they, or that there was any reason for it beyond the fact of this decision "in the counsels of eternity." I have no desire to be made so marked an exception to "the wrath of God." I am glad to cast in my lot with the great mass of intelligent believers in and practisers of goodness. I desire no better future than what they deserve, and what a just God would give them. I feel like apologizing for having wronged them in the past, by estimating some of the best and noblest of earth as being among the damned. I feel a true brotherhood with all men now. I am not one of the house of peers whom God has chosen to monopolize future happiness, but I am one of the great mass of men who are eagerly searching to know the right, believe the true, and do the good; and my future is safe, no matter how unable my intellect is to grasp the dogmas of the "Christian Fathers." A sense of companionship with good men of all races and creeds gives a feeling of joy which membership with the "elect" fails to impart to an unselfish mind. No conscientious man can be truly happy except by ignoring the doctrine of future everlasting punishment; and, if it is true, it is wrong to ignore it.

The effect of "trust in God" is offset by "fear of God." A belief in a superintending Providence that arbitrarily decides the issues of life is not promotive of peace of mind. One never knows what the will of God may decree next, and an element of uncertainty is introduced into human affairs beyond the elements of cause and effect. The Christian labors with the dread that, at any moment, God may thwart his efforts in "love" or "wrath," and give the success to some scoundrel, apparently unworthy of favors. The rationalist believes that, unless some natural impediment occurs, his work will prosper. If it fails, it was the result of individual fault or human ignorance. He recognizes the present limits of man's knowledge and foresight, and works in submission to these restrictions; but he has no dread of an inexplicable miraculous upsetting of his plans. The true "peace of God that passeth understanding" lies in the recognition of law and order in the universe, never interfered with by arbitrary and irresponsible acts.

Christianity, when consistently interpreted, assures its followers of tribulation in this world, and the hopelessness of all efforts to advance the moral welfare of the human race. The teachings of Jesus and Paul are pessimistic. Things are to wax worse and worse till the coming of Christ to destroy the world, out of which he saves his chosen few. It is the Christian then who is without hope in the world. His consolations are wholly in another world, the existence of which has never been made apparent to any other sense than "faith,"—that is, imagination.

The believer in natural law and its continuous working through evolution has grand assurance of infinite progress and a hopeful future for his race.

One who has escaped from belief that God curses his children, damns just men, and waits to destroy the world in vengeance, and sees, instead, an Infinite Power working forever through uninterrupted cause and effect toward the increasing development of man in righteousness, knowledge, and control of the universe,—he possesses a consolation and inspiration that makes life worth living.

MATERIAL IMMORTALITY.

A DREAM.

I was walking hand in hand with a friend along the busy street of a large city. Unconscious of passers-by and with a pleasing sense of mutual understanding and sympathy, I easily uttered these thoughts :—

"We have a passion for usefulness. Each day, our chief desire is to have made others better and happier, and to have made a record upon the world that will last and produce ever-increasing results for good. Our hope of immortality is not for a life of ease or spiritual rapture, but for a career of unceasing beneficence.

"But suppose there is no distinct individual existence beyond this life, shall we not live materially? Matter is indestructible, and will exist forever. These atoms that compose our bodies have, therefore, eternal life. They will scatter about the universe and assume an infinite variety of forms, but our ownership of them and identity with them will never be erased. We profess to love good for its own sake, not for its results to ourselves. It is, therefore, a satisfaction now to think of the unending influence of our bodies, even though no pleasurable consciousness ever comes to us in eternity. Atoms from our bodies may in future be parts of the most beautiful flowers, the largest trees, the grandest mountains, valuable gems, powerful machinery, useful chemical combinations, the finest animals, the most beautiful women, the noblest men. We may be represented in all the most charming forms and grandest enterprises of the future.

" But it may be that mind and matter are not two distinct entities, and that mind is an eternal property of matter, and each atom is a living, conscious soul. The union of their sensations constitutes what we call our minds ; but, when separated, they may each still have consciousness, and feel an intelligent sensation of their surroundings. Suppose we thus live forever, having a distinct conscious existence in these numberless atoms, how is our life multiplied by death? And not only by death. Every seven years, our bodies are completely changed. Each moment, some atoms leave us and others join us. Think of the diffusion of a body in a long life! Who could count our existences! Perhaps these atoms are influenced by the characteristics of the body they join, and our high or low moral condition is thus perpetuated. What an inducement to strive for perfection, if our sensations are to be multiplied by millions of existences!"

"But," said my companion, "these atoms have been in other bodies before they were in ours. How can we claim that they represent us exclusively in the future?"

"Probably not exclusively," I replied. "Each atom may receive new characteristics from the organism it inhabits, and may become more or less adapted for future service by the latest influence. Each atom may represent the average of the condition of the human beings with which it has been associated. Perhaps, atoms passing through a series of bodies of the highest quality may combine into richer grass, heavier wheat, more vigorous plants, more active brains; and thus, as man improves, all else in nature will be benefited, and through man's elevation the bondage in which creation groans and travails will be changed into 'the glorious liberty of the children of God'; that is, perfection."

LIBERAL CONVICTIONS.

SOME say there is no excuse for the utterance of liberal views, as they merely destroy faith and give nothing in the place of it. They remove certain restraints and give license to the passions. The atrocities of the French Revolution are the favorite illustration of this argument. Addison says, *Spectator*, No. 186: "A believer may be excused by the most hardened atheist for endeavoring to make him a convert, because he does it with an eye to both their interests. The atheist is inexcusable who tries to gain over a believer, because he does not propose the doing himself or believer any good by such a conversion. Why will any man be so impertinently officious as to tell me all this (the prospect of a future state) is only fancy and delusion? If it is a dream, let me enjoy it, since it makes me both the happier and better man."

These reasons have opposed all progress in the past. If a building is unsafe, it may be torn down before the plans of the new edifice are wholly completed. If a beacon is false, let it be removed, even before the true light-house can be built. If a belief that God wrote the Bible is untrue, and is moreover debasing to the intellect, let it be overthrown. If it is false that God of his own free will has elected some to everlasting life, and left the vast multitude of his creatures to suffer endless torment in hell, and if these ideas are injurious to both mind and heart, destroy them! The sooner the better. The abolition of slavery was opposed by good and wise men, because freedom would lead to license. Did this idea stop the anti-slavery party? The event proved the truth of the objection. The ignorant negro became the prey of the politicians who wanted his vote; and, trusting in their promise that the government would give to each man forty acres of land and a mule, he abandoned himself to the license of laziness, which he considered the essence of "freedery," until the inexorable logic of hunger and suffering taught him that true freedom was liberty to work and do right. He soon learned the lesson; and the doubled production of the South and its good order now prove that freedom is not a curse.

The liberal does propose doing good to the believer. He claims that all error is hurtful, and had better be abandoned. He believes that truth always works for good in the end, and can be safely left to take care of itself. He has not got to build a track for truth to run on. The men, who now are restrained from evil only by servile fear, may "have their fling" when these bonds are removed; but, in the school of experience, they would soon learn the utility of goodness, and be better men when they have learned to do well for higher motives than the dread of hell. If the motive is only the present good of themselves and others, it is a far better one. Goldsmith, in the "Vicar of Wakefield," says "that virtue which requires to be ever guarded is scarcely worth the sentinel."

But the advanced "higher life Christian," with whom the fear of future punishment is not an influence, but who from love to God delights to do his will, even he need fear no loss in motives: his devotion to *good* may continue, and his life be inspired by the same high enthusiasm. The name of his object of adoration will be only altered by the addition of one letter; and while retaining all that is desirable in his conception of the first, he will add to it utility and the impossibility of critical detraction. Whoever promotes the *good* blesses the human race: whoever praises *God* flatters an imagined existence, whose receipt of benefit can never be proved.

We, therefore, do not shrink from endeavoring to destroy faith in the dogmas of Christian theology, because we are convinced that belief in the Bible story of creation, which hindered the ideas of Copernicus and Galileo, and has opposed all progress of "earth knowledge" in the past, still prevents the intellectual growth of man, and the improvement of his circumstances by the discovery of the laws regulating the forces of nature.

The works of Darwin, Wallace, Tyndall, Huxley, and others, are called "the miserable speculations of infidel scientists"; their books will not be read, and, when one is urged to read the writings of the greatest men of our age, it is answered, "Moses and Paul are my great men." The devout and intense Christian pietists of to-day do not dare to read scientific books, lest their faith should be shaken, and these should prove more than a match for the writings of the Holy Ghost. They say: "There is nothing positive about the so-called discoveries of science. Sir John Lubbock now has contradicted Richard Proctor's theory that the earth will grow cold. We will wait until science comes back to Moses, as it is sure to do." Those who remove this barrier to the advance of knowledge are doing *good* service, though accused of not doing God service.

We are convinced that a belief that all the atrocious cruelties of the Hebrew wars, which those barbarous Israelites endeavored to excuse themselves for, by attributing them to the command of God, were really sanctioned and ordered by a being of infinite perfection, is injurious to morals, and has been the warrant for untold butcheries committed during wars waged in the name of God. No one need hesitate to destroy that dogma through fear that the world will grow worse, if its "restraint" is removed.

We are convinced that a belief in all the wonder tales of the Bible, which are paralleled or improved upon in every literature, keeps the mind in a childish condition; and that it is necessary to mental growth that the Hebrew fables and fairy tales should be placed where the myths of all other nations have already been put by intelligent men. Credulity has been slow in dying, but that is all the more reason why the loosening of its puerile "restraint" should be hastened. How can mankind be hurt by believing that Samson and Joshua and Jonah are brethren of Hercules and Agamemnon and Arion?

We are convinced that the sublime or raving utterances of Hebrew prophets are not God's vehicle of communicating the events of the future to this generation, and the belief that it is so leads to a vast waste of intellectual effort in sophistical reasoning and crazy imagination. It has been a curse to the human mind, giving men a low standard of the mind and nature of a God who was anxious to reveal something to them, and could find no better way of doing it than through disgusting symbols and unintelligible rhapsodies. This "restraint" can well be spared, and the reaction from mysticism to light will not make men stumble.

We are convinced that the assertion that the books of the New Testament are the genuine authentic writings of men inspired by the Holy Ghost, and therefore incapable of error, is not only false, but positively injurious; for the evidences are mainly drawn from the obscure, doubtful, garbled, and contradictory writings of fallible and often ignorant and credulous men, called Christian Fathers. The investigation of these evidences is impossible except to a few scholars; and it has made the great body of Christians the intellectual slaves of a hierarchy, who in the past have taken advantage of their power to impose all manner of dogmas and miracles upon the belief of their followers, in the name of the Christian Fathers. God will reveal himself to *me*, when he wants me to know something, and not imperil my reception of "the pure truth" by letting it roll around the cells and garrets of superstition, until prescribed to me by a learned doctor as the real and only genuine remedy; and I must swallow it on his authority, or die eternally. Men will only truly think for themselves when they learn that the evidences of "God's truth" are all around them, not in musty manuscripts, copied, altered, erased, defaced, and "restored," but in the glorious book of nature, which admits of no forgery, no erasure, no lie. This "restraint" it is safe to the intellect to remove.

We are convinced that the story of the life of Jesus is largely composed of the traditions of a credulous age; that his resurrection and ascension are mere myths; that the historical evidence of his existence is very meagre, and is entirely opposed to the prominence given to him in the New Testament. The passages chiefly relied upon in the works of contemporary historians to prove his life are now admitted to be forgeries, notably the passage in Josephus. The various Epistles may be genuine or not: the evidence is so conflicting, except for a few of Paul's Epistles, that no one should be asked to let his eternal salvation rest upon them. The writers were fallible men, and their unsupported testimony is not sufficient to prove the miraculous against the experience of the world. It is easier to believe they were mistaken. All that is good for restraint still remains to us, and needs no authority of " inspiration " to enforce it.

We are convinced that it is contrary to all moral ideas to teach that the guilty may be pardoned, because the innocent have suffered. The idea of the sacrifice of life, whether of brute or man, for "the salvation of souls," is a wicked and hurtful notion. It has led to countless atrocities, and still works evil, leading the Pocasset Christian to strike his knife to the heart of his little girl, and probably influencing the assassin of the President in his wicked deed. Jesus was put to death by the Jews on the charge of sedition and blasphemy. He tried to avoid it, but was betrayed by Judas. How this can be made an offering by God of his son for the sins of the world is past comprehension. We have no fear that men will be worse, if they lose the restraint of the idea that God, in all ages, has demanded the blood of the innocent as the condition of forgiveness of the guilty.

We are convinced that the doctrine of hell is an atrocious slander upon the character of God, and is not generally believed by thinking men in its connection with people that they know. An eminent orthodox minister, the head of a theological seminary, lately said to a circle of friends, "I do not believe the doctrine of eternal punishment, and I do not know a man who does." And yet it stands in the creeds, and men profess to believe it! A degraded idea of God is degrading to man, for "like master, like man." Though it has had some restraining influence in the past, the dread of hell exercises but little restraint now upon thinking men; and, where it acts, it is an unworthy motive, and produces servility. It has been the warrant for torture and massacre all through the ages; for may not men do just a little of what God does a good deal? If the Bible does not teach it, then God's word has misled his people for eighteen centuries; and the Holy Ghost has been "leading into all" error, and it is not a safe guide, for the next generation may prove it spoke falsely to us about something else.

We are convinced that the Bible teaching, as to

the present and future condition of the world, is utterly subversive of progress, and that all improvement is made in spite of it. Christians do not generally believe it now, because it is so repugnant to modern intelligence; but there it is in the Bible. All Christians used to believe it, and some do still. Things are to wax worse and worse, so that Jesus asks, "When the Son of Man cometh, shall he find faith on the earth?" The world, and all that is therein, shall be burned up. The early Christians, therefore, sought "a city that had foundations," and taught the despising and forsaking of this world. When this restraint is removed, men will become better citizens; and, feeling that they are not working merely to feed the flames of judgment, they will show more enthusiasm about improving the world.

We are convinced that all belief in the miraculous is a drag upon men's efforts, and enfeebling to their minds. Instead of trusting to prayer and ignoring the glorious faculties men possess, this restraint disappearing, each will strive "to do his level best," and feel there is no region into which his mind may not probe, and, proving all things, hold fast only that which he sees for himself is good.

Jesus promised that the Holy Spirit should lead his disciples into all truth, but his followers have differed and quarrelled ever since. He promised that prayer in his name should be answered, but the failures have at least equalled the fulfilments. He led his followers to expect his return to earth during their lifetime, but the hope proved fruitless. This disproves his infallibility.

These are points upon which all readers of the Bible can judge for themselves. We find that many scholars regard these stories as legendary: we may not be learned enough to weigh the evidence of this for ourselves, but, as their conclusion agrees with the internal evidences above mentioned, it appears the most plausible. While a respectable number of learned men on scholarly grounds deny the authenticity and genuineness of the Gospels, we are warranted in rejecting any of the doctrines taught therein which our reason disapproves.

In renouncing the errors of theology, do we give up anything that is valuable in Christianity, or that the moral sense of the world pronounces good? A thousand times no. We throw overboard the pagan rubbish and barbarous superstition that have incrusted the truth, that men have discovered in ages of experience of joy and sorrow, or, in other words, of good and evil. The truth remains to all. Christianity has never had a monopoly of it, and theologians do not control it now. We lose no hold of "love, joy, peace, long-suffering, gentleness, goodness, faith, meekness, temperance"; but we elevate them from the sphere of bondage to that of liberty.

REFORM.

However men may differ in theories concerning the past and the future, they are substantially agreed as to the practical needs of the present. A great problem faces us, the improvement of the world. The men of science, by study of nature's methods, are assisting material progress; but the sinfulness or imperfection of man is ever apparent, and good men of every religious creed and those who have no creed are alike striving to make men better individually, and to improve their social conditions. This motive has been supposed to be monopolized by religious people; and the common taunt to the unbeliever, when argument fails, is still, Your ideas are only destructive, and constructive ideas are what the world wants. But it has to be admitted that unbelievers are among the chief promoters of the welfare of society; and the candid observer must confess that all good men, Christian and Agnostic alike, in the concerns of this world, are united toward one practical end. All see the evils of crime, intemperance, and poverty, and equally desire to alleviate them. The difference between the workers is not in their aims, but in their methods. Christians seek reform supernaturally: rationalists seek it naturally.

The demand for constructive effort is a just one; and, if radicalism only tears down, it lacks the element that will commend it enduringly to society. Let us see if the methods of the rationalist will compare with those of the Christian. The cross of Christ is the great remedy of the Christian. If a man is evil, he is taught that, by an emotional consideration of the death of Jesus, a supernatural change is wrought upon his nature, which will enable him to be good henceforth. This effect is often produced, and in many cases is lasting; but more often, when the emotion has subsided, evil practices are resumed. Under the stimulus of the love of Christ, men resolve to reform their lives; but feeling declines, and temptations conquer. Has the rationalist a better method of reform? He believes that reason is a more lasting influence than emotion; that the prospect of present benefit is more potent than the hope of future reward; that, as material progress is gained by the study of nature, so moral and mental advance is to come by the study of man's history and habits, and by observation of nature's methods of development. He sees that evil arises from ignorance of natural law, or from non-conformity to its teachings. Therefore, the remedy is suggested by the cause. Knowledge of "man's place in nature," and understanding of the physical forces that affect his welfare will supply the sources of improvement.

Education, then, is the remedy of the rationalist: regeneration is the remedy of the Christian. The latter has had a long trial, and has doubtless won trophies. The very fact of its birth and continuance proves that it had some adaptedness to the circumstances that called it forth from men's minds, and it has been serviceable under the existing conditions in the past. Its success, however, is not such as to commend it as a panacea for ill, nor for any application in the future to intelligent minds. Ignorance is alike the mother of devotion and the mother of crime. The least instructed people are the most religious and the most vicious. Lange, in " History of Materialism," says, " Enlightenment and education, as a rule, go hand in hand with a decrease of the clergy in relative numbers and influence"; and "the diminution of crime corresponds with the diminution of superstition, which is inseparably connected with the worship of the letter."

Education in a broad sense is of recent birth, and is yet in its infancy; yet its fruits are undeniably good. Instruction has been limited to the acquisition of ancient ideas; but, since three hundred years past, it has been gradually expanding to embrace what the Germans call "earth knowledge," which is gained by direct study of nature's operations and conditions. Social progress is coincident with this advance.

But let us apply these principles to the vexed questions of the day, and see which method is best adapted to reform. The most prominent topics of concern are capital and labor, intemperance, crime, and the relations of the sexes. What is the Christian method of dealing with poverty? By Christian, we mean the methods taught in the New Testament. Intelligent Christians have generally abandoned these and adopt rational methods, but they have no right to credit these to Christianity. Jesus and the apostles, in view of the expected closing of the age, commended poverty, rebuked riches, ordered the distribution of wealth, the lending of money without asking for repayment, and the practice of communism. Rationalists say poverty is a curse, strive to gain riches, secure your individual comfort, keep your possessions except when you can do more good by parting with them; giving degrades the receiver, and injures his future efficiency; nature teaches "nothing without labor," and men must toil for what they would enjoy. But they see also the interdependence of men, that true self-interest demands the advancement of one's neighbor, that the employer's welfare is promoted by the prosperity of the employed, that a grasping selfishness injures him who exercises it, and they would educate men to far-seeing views of trade and wealth. They would show that nature indicates that general prosperity is promoted by freedom of trade, co-operation in production, the discouragement of pauperism by the promotion of inducements to industry, and thus by purely material considerations they would lead to prosperity rather than by abstract didactic inculcations based upon self-sacrifice through devotion to Jesus. They claim that the more nature's methods are studied the more clearly it is shown that the truth and lasting welfare of each individual is identical with the welfare of the community in which he dwells, and that the prosperity of each community is connected with the thrift of other communities. They believe that enlarged knowledge will promote a more efficient benevolence springing from motives of worldly self-interest than has been obtained by the principle of self-sacrifice for a heavenly crown or through emotional "love of God."

Intemperance is consistently combated by the Christian through conversion and prohibition. Drunkards are reclaimed by the stimulus of consecrated vows and by the impossibility of indulgence. But both experiences are rare. The vows lose force, and seeming impossibilities are overcome. The means of intoxication are procured by liquors or by opiates, where the craving has become confirmed. The rational method is to allow individual freedom, but to aim at prevention by the spread of knowledge of the evil effects of ardent spirits, by the inculcation of self-restraint for the advantage of self and others, and by study of the laws of heredity which may suggest means of preventing the transmission of depraved appetites. The recognition of intemperance as a disease, and its treatment by scientific methods, is in brief the method of rationalism.

As to crime, the same remarks may largely apply. The science of heredity has a great mission in this field. Conversion may rescue a few; but the improvement of the race must be gradually effected by physical improvement, by vivid impressions of the certainty of the punishment of crime, and by the growth of prosperity. A disciple asked the ancient rationalist, Confucius, "Since the people are so numerous, what more is needed?" Confucius replied, "Make them well off." "After that, what else?" "Instruct them." Preaching and tracts will not restrain the starving. Comfort is a prerequisite to learning. The question of capital and labor is therefore a problem intimately connected with that of crime, and general thrift must precede general virtue.

The relation of the sexes is a question made more difficult of solution, because a false propriety restricts its discussion. With this as with the other problems, the rationalist has no patent nostrums to effect immediate cures; but he claims to point out the methods in which light may best be gained. The present attitude of Christianity upon this topic is that of positive, unreasoning dictation. Thou shalt not,—because Moses and Christ said so. Look to Jesus for strength to conquer fleshly lusts. "Deny thyself, and take thy cross!" The failure of this method need not be argued. The method of rationalism would be the spread of knowledge about the human body; the recognition of the fact that there is nothing unholy or unclean in our organisms or natural impulses; the removal of a false glamour and exaggerated notions, that the sexes entertain toward each other, by co-education and familiar association; early instruction upon the direful effects of sexual vices, and demonstration that self-control is the truest self-interest. A refined lady graduate of a Western college, where co-education of the sexes was practised, remarked: "Whenever I met friends who were being educated in young ladies' seminaries, they usually talked about the young men and their secret efforts to correspond or associate with them: whereas our daily association with young men showed us what commonplace and often stupid things they were. They had no exaggerated fascination for us, and I am sure there was less 'flirting' than where the girls were secluded."

One who faces the ills of life, the woes of the wretched, the sorrows and "sins" of men, is at times overwhelmed with the consciousness of the hopelessness of speedy amelioration. He can only ask himself what general principles are best adapted to furnish remedies; and he finds two suggestions,—Christian supernaturalism and rational naturalism. But he says, if God can remedy all this, why doesn't he do it? Men have been pleading for ages for him to fulfil his promise to answer prayer, and to heed their petitions that these ills should be removed. He has had opportunity to prove his power and faithfulness, but he has failed to effect the desired reforms. On the other hand, it is seen that all permanent progress has been secured by natural agencies, and the past reveals the future.

We claim, therefore, that not only does rationalism refute the charge that it is solely destructive, but all valuable construction is secured by its methods. Where Christianity influences intelligent people for good, it is owing to its adoption of rationalism. Its modified supernaturalism is serviceable to some heathen races as a stepping-stone toward naturalism; but the motive forces that advance civilization are not prayer, conversion, and religious dogmas, but knowledge of nature and the application of her hitherto secret powers to the welfare of man.

Education, then, must consist less in the study of dead languages and dying theologies, and more in research into nature's operations and the endeavor to conform our lives to those beneficent principles that underlie her methods.

TRUTH IN ERROR.

I. HELL.

It may be asserted that all universal beliefs have either been founded upon some genuine fact of nature or have been serviceable in the development of man. They may have been to a great extent mistaken inferences, but there was a basis of truth and a measurably beneficial result. When more of the fact is discovered, man's conceptions change, and he alters his belief and his methods. In rejecting the religious dogmas, whose falsity is being exposed by the increasing light of science, we do well to search if there is any good thing in them and preserve the truth germs they may contain, which have been helpful to man in the past, remembering Shakespeare's words,—

> "There is some soul of goodness in things evil,
> Would men observingly distill it out."

One of the most prominent universal beliefs is that of punishment after death, which in Calvinism has assumed the form of the doctrine of the eternal torment in hell of all who reject the way of salvation by the atonement of Christ. The falsity of this dogma has often been shown; but its opponents do not always recognize the fact that its belief rests upon a fundamental truth, which is, that the law of the unfailing succession of cause and effect prevails in morals as truly as in the physical world.

It is considered a waste of words to attack the Calvinistic doctrine of endless punishment, for it may fairly be claimed that no intelligent person now believes it. True, many profess to believe it, and some even think they believe it; but, judged by accepted rules of evidence, their belief is disproved. Genuine belief is always manifested in corresponding action. Belief in the existence of a pitfall, the approach of an avalanche, or the presence of a wild beast, is always eagerly communicated to others. Men will not allow others to go into danger without warning and without deep concern for their welfare. Judged by this rule, how many really believe the doctrine of everlasting punishment? If men all around us are going down to an eternal hell, and Christians believe it and know of an easy way of escape, would they so seldom vary their lives of business and pleasure by a word to the impenitent? Would they be able to live contentedly in a round of diversion, music, embroidery, and cigar-smoking, while their neighbors are dropping into ceaseless doom, where "the smoke of their torment ascendeth up for ever and ever"? Would ministers of churches only make vague allusions to the dread dogma, and leave the preaching of terror to evangelists, without charge of societies, who are not imperilled by the dissent of parishioners? It is seldom preached now in city churches, and ministers' minds are everywhere perplexed in the effort to reconcile revelation with good taste.

Genuine belief is evidenced not only by action, but also by a consistent application of the theory espoused. But the doctrine of eternal damnation is never applied within the circle of the believer's acquaintance; it only does for strangers and heathen, or possibly, like Artemas Ward, for one's wife's relations. In all cases where sympathy is aroused, it is denied or evaded. A lady, brought up in this creed, professedly held to it, until a favorite son, a wild, wayward boy, swam across a stream to rob an orchard, and, being chased by the owner, was drowned in mid stream, with profane curses on his lips. Her creed sent him to hell; but the loving mother's heart abolished the creed, and she ceased to be a Calvinist.

Two ladies, cousins, lived alongside of each other in a sea-port town. One was brought up as a Calvinist, the other as a Unitarian. They were wealthy, intelligent, hospitable, and especially kind to the poor. They lived to old age, and died,— one trusting in Christ for salvation through his atoning blood, the other, without any faith in

Christ, peacefully committing her soul into the hands of her heavenly Father. A lady who was a cousin of both was asked, "Can any one be saved who rejects Christ as an atoning Saviour?"

She emphatically answered, "No; the Bible clearly says so: 'He that believeth not the Son shall not see life, but the wrath of God abideth on him.'"

"Did your cousin S. believe in Christ as a Saviour?"

"No, she died as she lived, denying that he was anything more than a good man."

"Then, she is in hell!"

She started in horror, and replied: "Oh, she was a dear good soul! It can't be!"

Let us see what the doctrine of hell means, when consistently applied. The population of the world is stated to be 1,350,000,000. Of these, about 300,000,000 are nominal Christians; but very few have been converted or born again, and, "except a man be born again, he cannot see the kingdom of God." The majority rely for salvation upon the rites of the church or good works, or else are indifferent as to their future state. An estimable and learned man has lately said in a public lecture that, of those whom men call Christians, God would only call two per cent. Christians. Upon this estimate there are six million truly converted Christians in the world; and, as about forty million people die every year, it follows logically that yearly 180,000 people go to heaven, and 39,820,000 are doomed to hell. There have been many people who would have assented to this, and who had no hope for the salvation of infants and heathen; but the mind and heart of the nineteenth century revolt from these atrocious statements. Infant salvation is now generally admitted, except that Roman Catholics limit salvation to the baptized. This rescues half of the human race; and charity saves a majority of the rest, in fact all toward whom sentiment is excited. Men will not now admit there are few that be saved, though they still profess to revere the words of Jesus,— "few are chosen," and "few there be that find it." To make the doctrine less horrible, some say that the unbelieving are annihilated. They find this in the Bible, but the great majority of Christians do not so read it. Others say the heathen will not perish: but, to justify foreign missions, Prof. Shedd preached a sermon before the American Board, entitled "The Guilt of the Pagan," enforcing Paul's words, "For as many as have sinned without law shall also perish without law"; and he proved that, according to the Scriptures, the heathen are "without excuse." The Broad Churchman relies upon Canon Farrar's interpretation of *aionios* and *gehenna* to soften the doctrine and limit the duration of the penalty.

But none of these explanations reconcile the reflecting mind and tender heart to the docrine of damnation as being the will and revelation of God. An eminent Congregational minister was asked what he thought about eternal punishment. "I try never to think of it," was replied. "If I do, it gives me the blues for a fortnight." When an unregenerate philanthropist dies, men fall back upon "the mercy of God," and say, "Shall not the judge of all the earth do right!" "None will perish without a good reason for it." "We know not what may have passed between the soul and its Saviour in the last moments." Carlyle, Emerson, Longfellow, and Darwin may reject revelation with impunity, but woe to the unknown and unhonored unbeliever!

A doctrine thus loosely believed is not worthy of attack, and we can only wonder that men do not abandon it in principle, as they have already done in practice. Instead of attempting to trim down the doctrine into accord with science and sense, thus conceding the imperfection of "revelation," is it not more honoring to God and more creditable to man to admit that the New Testament contains merely the human record of the human beliefs of the age in which it was written?

But is this all-prevailing idea of hell, reaching over all lands and back through distant ages, utterly false? No: it is founded on fact and use.

as is every other human belief. The fact is the pleasurableness of good and the painfulness of evil. In the long run, virtue brings its own reward and sin its own curse; and these results continue while existence lasts. The sinner will forever be the worse off for his sin: no atonement, no death-bed repentance, can remove the natural consequences of sin to the guilty. It is untrue that a complete and hopeless doom will be arbitrarily inflicted upon the sinner; but the natural ill of each transgression will follow its commission. Nature has recuperative power: the wound in the flesh is healed; but the effort has made a certain drain, minute it may be, upon the stock of vitality. So, evil in the end may sometimes lead to good, but there has been a loss that is never repaired. Men seem to escape the consequences of their evil acts; but a knowledge of their thoughts and lives would show the ills they bear, and these are often more plainly manifested in their posterity. This is the truth that underlies the false doctrine of hell,—natural retribution.

The use of the belief is the restraining power of fear. This has been a potent influence in the past; but the doubted threat loses its power, and men are losing belief in hell. It no longer terrifies educated people, and its far-away curse does not restrain the passionate.

Liberals are accused of lessening the restraints

upon immorality by overthrowing the Bible doctrine of everlasting punishment; but they really are more severe toward sin than are the orthodox, for they do not encourage the sinner to believe that the consequences of lifelong crimes can be escaped by the lifting of the eye to the cross. They teach unavoidable injury from sin.

Though men cease to have the dread of eternal, hopeless torture before them, other motives may be as serviceable. The perception of the advantages of goodness, a sense which is growing in man through the experience of ages, the certainty of the human retribution of crime, which social science will yet evolve, and the perception of the inevitable natural punishment which follows all wrong-doing,—this hope and these fears will regenerate the world.

II. ATONEMENT AND SALVATION.

The doctrine of atonement, which pervades the Bible and exists in some form in all religions, the necessity of the suffering of one as the condition for the forgiveness of another, must have a basis of truth, or it could never have gained such wide acceptance throughout the world as it has done.

The Calvinistic doctrine of salvation by faith in Christ is impossible to understand, and harder still to believe, except by those who adopt the motto,

"I believe because it is impossible." Many different theories of the atonement are presented. The old school Calvinists believe in the sacrificial atonement, that Christ died in our stead, saving us by substitution, bearing the wrath of God that was due to us. A newer school, expounded by Dr. Bushnell, and fast growing in our theological seminaries, accepts the moral theory of the atonement, or various modifications of the idea of vicarious atonement approaching to the moral theory, which makes the life and death of Christ efficacious only as an example, and makes salvation the act of the grace of God, not purchased by Christ's suffering. We are told to believe in Christ in order to be saved, but what we are to believe about Christ is so variously stated that the seeker is bewildered.

This is a most unsatisfactory doctrine to attack, for, whatever phase of atonement is controverted, the assailant is told he has misconceived the theory; and, if he patiently demolishes every aspect in turn, it is said that our only concern is to have faith in the person of Christ, and how he saves us, and in what way God looks upon the atonement as accomplishing this, God only knows.

This doctrine teaches us that the penitent thief upon the cross, the believing murderer on the scaffold, the dying aged sinner converted in his last illness, do, upon their deaths, immediately pass into glory; but the rational philanthropist, the earnest laborious scientist, or good moralist, of sceptical minds, after long lives of devotion to the welfare and elevation of the human race, must perish eternally.

Belief is largely accidental: the children of believers are apt to believe, the children of sceptics doubt. Comparatively few leave the creed they were brought up to profess: therefore, the children are punished for the parents' sin to remote generations. This idea universal morality condemns.

Children are seldom converted until they are twelve or fifteen years of age. What becomes of those who die earlier, a large proportion of the human race? Baptismal regeneration provides for their safety. But Calvinists reject that dogma, and make no definite logical provision for their salvation. They rest in a vague idea that God gives the benefit of the atonement to those who are not responsible for the choice; but they have never decided at what age a child becomes responsible, and the sorrowing parents must wait till eternity to know whether their children have received a free pass into heaven on account of their youth or idiocy, or have been rejected as responsible beings.

Although, in practical morality, men condemn the imposition of suffering upon the innocent in order to spare the guilty, and declare that the righteousness of one cannot offset the sin of another, yet they become familiar with voluntary sacrifice for the temporal good of others. "Nothing without labor" is a natural law. Toil for money, study for learning, exercise for strength, self-denial for benevolence, are some of the labors endured for desired results. It is observed in all life that trial and suffering are the price of advancement, and that the joy of one is promoted by the calamity of another. Men die to save other men from drowning or burning, and to preserve the liberties of their race. In nature there is not only a struggle for existence and a survival of the fittest, but on every side we see self-sacrifice for the good of others, and benefits springing from misfortunes. The parent animals devote their lives to the rearing of their young. Each order of animals dies for the sustenance of a higher race. The falling leaf and decaying tree fertilize the ground for new growths. These may be the foundation facts which men have transferred to the sphere of morals.

If the theory of eternal salvation through another's sufferings be abandoned, the fact of the possibility of the present salvation of men through our own efforts remains. Perhaps laziness and selfishness have had something to do with putting salvation upon God instead of upon our own labors, just as Sydney Smith described English benevolence, saying, "When A sees B in distress, he has a strong desire to compel C to help him." It is easier to say "God help you" than to lend a hand to a suffering brother. We may all be saviors, offering up ourselves daily for the good of others; and, by another law of nature, we shall find that such offering blesses him who gives.

Each person who endures an ill may feel that he has borne it for some one else; for only a certain proportion of accidents happen, and each one who is a victim spares another from the affliction, and thus makes atonement for him.

III. THE GOD OF THE BIBLE.

The Bible bears the marks of having been written by sincere men. They were sometimes credulous, superstitious, and ignorant, as judged by present standards, and their writings are therefore cumbered with legend, myth, and mistake; but back of all lies truth, and every dogma has some foundation principle which we do well to recognize.

The personal Jehovah, who wars, hates, and kills, sends famines and pestilences, and creates evil,— who also creates life, loves, blesses, and forgives, —is a human conception of the mind, soul, principle, law, force, or we may say God, that works in matter, and produces all things material and mental by orderly development. Our reverence for this principle is only increased by denuding it of its human attributes; and we only change Gods, as men in every age and clime have done as their knowledge of nature has altered.

We are nearer to the foundation truth by this change, but the mystery of eternal existence without beginning is unsolved. If we cannot define this God in human phrase, it yet calls out every attribute of wonder, reverence, and aspiration in our natures. It is a far greater marvel than the Hebrew Deity or Calvin's God, and more worthy of respect.

We can see its working in the blade of grass and the forest tree, in the summer breeze and the tornado, in the calm of evening twilight and the earthquake,—not by phenomenal and arbitrary acts, but through a procession of causes reaching back beyond mortal ken. Pain and destruction are not the deliberate acts of a wrathful or chastening God, who consciously sends them with reference to their immediate effects; but they are the necessary results of an eternal succession of causes. And we do not need to propitiate the Deity that he may not send such calamities, but we need to increase our knowledge of these operations of nature, that, by coming into harmony with their workings, we may avoid their evil results. Each disaster is a factor in man's education; and experience will, in future ages, lead to his triumph over evil. The loss of life in burning buildings, instead of leading us to implore God to avert such disasters in future, teaches us to use new precautions against fire, and make improved exits. It is a great relief to feel that we are not under the discipline of a ruler who is to be propitiated by our mental exercises, but to know that the forces that now control us are merely teaching us how to become their masters.

Our reverence is called forth by this tendency toward goodness which pervades nature, whatever its origin; and our aspiration is stimulated to let our lives come into harmony with nature's methods, and let both joy and sorrow promote our own good and that of others.

IV. CONVERSION.

The Calvinistic theory of conversion is only the exaggerated form of a vital truth. Conversion, on its natural side, is repentance and reform, the resolve to cease from violations of natural laws, and conform our lives to a standard of right-doing which is approved by reason and conscience. These turnings about and intense resolutions to follow goodness are manifested under all religions, and will both exist and increase when their naturalness is recognized. The emotional, frenzied, and "supernatural" side of conversion is also common to all religions and climes, and is a natural effect of the intense concentration of the mind upon a given subject. This form of orthodox conversion seldom occurs to persons who have reached the age of maturity. It is supposed they have become hardened in their sins, and cannot change. But they do all their best work then in every other branch of knowledge; and why should not their estimate of religion be equally valuable? The true explanation is that theology rests upon emotion and human authority, not upon reason. Suppose a teacher proclaimed a new law of physics, and nine-tenths of all his converts were under twenty-one years of age, would not this fact be deemed strong evidence against the value of his theory?

The sudden resolution to forsake evil and choose good, called conversion, will continue to be exercised, even if belief in the supernatural is abanoned.

V. ELECTION.

The doctrine of election, that God of his own good pleasure, from all eternity, has elected some to everlasting life, produces a hurtful conceit in the elect and an uncharitable assumption in their conduct toward sinners. They imagine the existence of a supernatural difference between themselves and other men, and hold aloof from them or patronize them offensively. If God should neglect to save them, why should we trouble ourselves about it? If God can send numbers of men to hell every day, why, if he can stand it, we can! Does not this blunt sensibility, paralyze effort and hinder the brotherhood of man? This arbitrary choice of men to be saved is irrational and immoral; and yet it is the perverted form of one of the most vital truths of nature,—the survival of the fittest,—the fact that fitness finds its sphere. If one is qualified for action or service, the opportunity is apt to come to him, the occasion seeks the man. Thus there is a natural selection, leading to the triumph of the best. The true "elect" are the discoverers, the searchers, the earnest laborers, who in science, morals, education, and benevolence, are quietly but surely redeeming the world. These are "the chosen ones," "the peculiar people zealous of good works." Every creed is on their lips; but their purpose is one, and their reward cometh.

VI. THE MILLENNIUM.

The hope of a brighter future, a perfect day for the world, has had a place in the mythologies of almost all nations. The Greeks and Romans, while lamenting the decline of the world from the Golden Age in which it commenced, comforted themselves with the assurance of its restoration.

The Persians expected the triumph of Ormuzd over Ahriman and the consequent overthrow of all ill. The Jews and Christians, in their millennium or thousand years of blessedness, have only voiced again the yearning and hope of humanity for a blessed era of peace, prosperity, righteousness, and happiness.

If universal beliefs have a basis of truth, it may be asked whether science gives any intimation of a foundation fact for this universal hope of "a good time coming."

Research of the past and observation of the present reveal *progress*, and when this is recognized hope seizes upon the fact as a promise of perfection. Not only in history do we see a growth upward in man's development in morals, knowledge, and arts, but study of the earth reveals an upward progression in life. The earliest stratified rocks show us only the remains of the lowest forms of animal and plant life, and in successive later deposits come the higher orders of life. Haeckel divides the history of life upon the earth, as shown by the testimony of the rocks, into five great epochs in which life developed in an ascending scale, in the following order: 1. Skulless vertebrates and seaweeds; 2. Fishes and ferns; 3. Reptiles and pines; 4. Mammals and leaf forests; 5. Man and cultivated forests. The earth tells this story of progress, and analogy asks, Why should progress stop short of perfection? A development of matter from moneron to man gives warrant for all the fondest dreams of the future development of life into angelic forms, and of the enlargement of man's powers to godlike efficiency. If atom develops to man, man may advance to God.

The early Christians believed this Golden Age to be "at hand," and many now look for the speedy coming of the Lord and the deliverance of the groaning creation into "the glorious liberty of the sons of God." It may be asked, If science admits the probability of a state of future blessedness upon the earth, what has it to say of times and seasons? Here again the analogies of the past prompt the hope that the day of promise "draweth nigh."

Haeckel estimates that the life-bearing rocks, which have been deposited in strata by the waters have a thickness of about one hundred and thirty thousand feet. The strata bearing the low forms of the first epoch are about seventy thousand feet, or more than half the whole thickness. The strata of the second period—that of fishes and ferns—are considered to be about forty-two thousand feet thick, or one-third of the whole. The third period—the reptile and pine era—shows strata fifteen thousand feet thick, or one-ninth of the whole. The fourth epoch—the age of mammals—

shows only three thousand feet of rock, or one-fortieth of the whole. And the strata of the fifth epoch—or age of man—are but one two hundredth part of the whole life-bearing strata of rocks. Thus the brevity of the past periods of development appears in the ratio of 2, 3, 9, 40, 200. From this we learn that, as forms become higher, the period of development has shortened; and a continuance of this process will evolve a continually hastening change to higher and better things.

In our observation of society, we observe the rapid improvement made in many departments of life by one invention. We see how benefits act and interact in constantly growing proportions, and influence spheres never contemplated in their origin. We see material forces promoting moral progress, as when railroads and telegraphs assist the detection and therefore the repression of crime. Each advance promotes activity in thousands of channels, and the progress of development is continually accelerated.

Thus the analogies of the past excite the expectation of constantly shortening epochs of advancement, and Science proclaims the glad tidings that "the coming of the Lord draweth nigh," "the night is far spent, the day is at hand." A better and brighter day for humanity approaches with ever quickening footsteps, and promises a career to man unlimited by harps and crowns, but leading ever on to infinite attainment.

VII. CHRISTIANITY.

There is nothing in Christianity that is recognized generally as good, which is lost or weakened in any way by the renunciation of its encircling superstition. Jesus may still be to us an ideal of human goodness, an example of many virtues, though stripped of what scientific criticism shows to be the accretions of credulous tradition. He was divine in nature, as all men are,—the highest products of the inscrutable force that has moved in matter till it flowered into humanity.

The Holy Spirit dwells in every unbeliever in his personality, who does not grieve him away by an evil life that debases him too low to experience an enthusiasm for goodness; and who ever sinks to this depth? It is a false assumption that this divine influence only comes to believers in a certain theory. The true holy spirit is the impulse "to do justly, love mercy, and make other men happy," which dwells in some measure in the breast of every man, of every race, and every land, and which grows as it is exercised and as true knowledge increases.

All existence is a miracle. Revelation is continually given to the earnest student of nature.

The inventor, the scholar, and the philanthropist are inspired. Rewards and punishments follow naturally upon causes. Heaven comes to bless the successful effort and lofty endeavor, bestowing as natural results present happiness on the striver and future good to his race. Hell curses the inefficient, immoral, and unnatural, bringing sorrow and pain to the evil or unwise doer and extending resulting miseries to the race. A persistent continuance in well-doing leads upward to sanctification and holiness; and habits of goodness become so confirmed that falling from grace becomes improbable, and the perseverance of saints is assured.

We are not undermining the building of goodness, or sapping the tree of virtue, by destroying Calvinism or Christianity or Judaism. We only tear down the decayed parts of the superstructure built by men upon the foundation of eternal truth, and shake off the dead leaves and prune the rotten twigs from the branches of the tree of knowledge, in order that new structures may be reared and fresh growths may be promoted.

FREE THOUGHT RHYMES.

In days gone by, the people thought
That only what the clergy taught
   Was worthy of belief;
They held the keys of heaven's gate,
And knew the mysteries of fate,—
   Eternal joy or grief.

Now, men have learned that all may pry,
With open ear and eager eye,
   Throughout all nature's realm.
There's no monopoly of light,
And he is safe who does the right;
   For Law controls the helm.

'Twas said that God from naught made earth,
And gave to varied life its birth
   Within six solar days;
He made things all at once, complete,
All very good to his conceit,
   So marvellous were his ways.

But Science says, throughout the past
The world has grown, in ages vast,
   By nature's forward plan;
The whirling star dust formed the world,
And life by slow degrees unfurled
   From Moneron to Man.

'Twas said that erring man eat fruit,
When tempted by a talking brute ;
   God's curse upon him fell!
But mercy kept a chosen few,
For whom Christ's death should sin undo,
   And save their souls from hell.

But now we learn that man arose
From savage natures, and his foes
   By knowledge will be slain.
His path is ever up and on,
And conquests, by his study won,
   Redeem from ill and pain.

The railroad, telegraph, and press
Work mightily to render less
   Impunity of crime.
Extension of the reign of law
From evil deeds will men withdraw,
   And haste the Golden Time.

Man need not fear eternal wrath,
Nor vengeance lurking in his path,
   Should he presume to think.
But Nature gives her richest prize
To him who dares in search to rise
   And at her fountains drink.

Her works new revelations give,
A Bible that will ever live
   And shed increasing light;
Beyond the writings of the Jews
Her precepts blessedness diffuse,
   And teach the true and right.

Ye earnest men, no longer shrink
From speaking what you truly think;
   Proclaim the truth you find!
And let free search, free speech, free thought,
By blood of ancient worthies bought,
   Advance the human mind.

THE END.